Woodrow Wilson

Woodrow Wilson

USA

Brian Morton

First published in Great Britain in 2008 by
Haus Publishing Ltd
26 Cadogan Court
Draycott Avenue
London SW3 3BX
www.hauspublishing.com

A CIP catalogue record for this book
is available from the British Library

ISBN 978-1-905791-62-0

Series design by Susan Buchanan
Typeset in Sabon by MacGuru Ltd
Printed in Dubai by Oriental Press
Maps by Martin Lubikowski, ML Design, London

Contents

Acknowledgements

As well as to the many scholars who have taken on the life and multifarious writings of Woodrow Wilson, I owe an even longer-standing debt to Owen Dudley Edwards, Richard Crockatt, and Eric Homberger who were my mentors – if not my formal tutors – in American history and politics at the Universities of Edinburgh and East Anglia. I owe a great deal, too, to Geir Lundestad, currently director of the Norwegian Nobel Institute but a profound scholar of American civilisation, to whom I briefly and bizarrely stood as proxy at the University of Tromsø in 1979 while he fulfilled obligations elsewhere. It was a hugely fruitful experience, but homoeopathically cured me of any desire to be a lifelong academic.

Profound thanks to my commissioning editor Jaqueline Mitchell, who could have deployed more severe sanctions as this manuscript ran ever later but who kept channels of diplomacy open and avoided conflict. Brief thanks, too, to Gore Vidal who referred to Woodrow Wilson as 'idiotic' during a BBC interview, and rekindled my enthusiasm at a moment when health and spirits were at a low ebb.

I've counted, too, on the unswerving loyalty and support of my wife Sarah (whose brother Neil is in harm's way with the American Marines in Iraq at the time of writing) and our son John who will be pleased to see that books about the 'glasses man' are no longer cluttering his father's desk. And if it doesn't make me sound too much like a Miss World contestant, this essay is dedicated to world peace, which has never seemed to me a foolish or unworthy aim.

Woodrow Wilson with President Poincaré of France on his arrival in Paris in December 1918.

Introduction: *Dear ghosts ...*

Colorado is American heartland. High, semi-arid, landlocked, tucked between the great plains and the Continental Divide that runs down the middle of the Rocky Mountains, neither 'North' nor 'South' – the 'Centennial State' did not join the Union until a decade after the Civil War – Colorado retains a reputation for political independence, a folk-memory, perhaps, of the state's previous existence as a free Territory, self-determining and relatively unorganised. On 25 September 1919, a man came to the small south-eastern Colorado city of Pueblo, trying to save an idea.

The idea in its purest form was peace, but it was typical of a man still routinely and misleadingly described as an idealist, condemned by his enemies as a naïve and dangerous utopian, and still casually dismissed by history as a failure, that he should be more concerned to defend the form and practical structure of his idea than the idea itself. In Pueblo, Woodrow Wilson, 28th President of the United States, made his last public attempt to demonstrate that these things were inseparable and inextricable, and to convince the American people to accept in undiluted and uncompromised form both the Treaty of Versailles, which had brought to an end the

Great War in Europe, and a great international League of Nations as a guarantor of future peace. It is one of the great ironies of history that having expended extraordinary effort on both the treaty, of which he was a major architect, and the idea of a League – his name is indissolubly linked to the latter, though the first proposal came from an English statesman – and having sacrificed health and political standing at home to an insistence that they be adopted together and whole, he should repeatedly instruct his Democratic supporters in the Senate to vote against them both and deny acceptance of the Paris peace settlement and American entry into the League of Nations the two-thirds majority they needed for ratification.

The irony was widely perceived, then and since. In 1945, at the end of a second world conflict widely accepted as an inevitable extension of the first and a bloody confirmation of the misjudgements of the Paris Peace Conference and the disastrous consequences of American failure to ratify the treaty and join the League, the historian Thomas A Bailey published a book entitled *Woodrow Wilson and the Great Betrayal*. The title alone gives little indication who is doing the betraying or what is being betrayed, but a line from the book jumps out: 'With his own sickly hands, Wilson slew his own brain child.'[1] In 1919, a satirical cartoonist had anticipated the same metaphor, depicting a sombrely clad Wilson – always caricatured in clerical black – rocking a stillborn infant in a tiny coffin-cradle, while the British and French prime ministers David Lloyd George and Georges Clemenceau, fellow-architects of the Treaty, lurk ambiguously in the background.

Successive waves of revisionist historiography since his death in 1924 have attempted to vilify or rehabilitate Wilson, in terms that are either politically crude or psychologically hyper-subtle. Born in the same year as Sigmund Freud, it was

Wilson's ambiguous fate to be the first living political leader to be profiled (albeit at a distance) by the founder of psychoanalysis, in collusion with William C Bullitt, a Wilson aide at the Peace Conference who resigned over what he considered the severity of the terms being imposed on Germany.[2] Bullitt – whose name alone suggests potential for analysis in the circumstances – was one of many who felt that Wilson was betraying his own principles and promises. That is a perception that goes to the heart of the paradox, for Woodrow Wilson, whose politics altered the course of the 20th century and who almost single-handedly shaped the 'new world order', is an infinitely more subtle, more intellectually nuanced, more ruthless leader than the usual textbook versions suggest. At some level, Wilson does seem susceptible to reductionist explanations; one comparative biography casts him opposite Theodore Roosevelt as *The Warrior and the Priest*.[3] Some part of that is due to a remarkable and often overlooked foreshortening of the chronology. Wilson spent only nine years in national politics and only three on an international stage, and if his career seems given over to the promulgation of one Big Idea, that idea – and the apparatus that came with it – only occupied him for a tiny proportion of a life that very nearly reached its biblical span. To be sure, his actions – and in almost equal measure his refusals to act – during the period are of incalculable significance, but to concentrate on them entirely is to lose a vital context.

In the same way, to concentrate on Wilson's health and psychology, both of which have been analysed in unprecedented detail, is to miss a point as well. His background as a Presbyterian 'son of the manse' was an important shaping influence on his subsequent career, but the specific nature of that influence remains unclear, as does the impact of his mother's hypochondriasis, which he seems to have inherited. Some have seen this emerging even in his speeches, where health – of the nation, of the individual, of democracy – is a recurring metaphor, and the metaphor in turn reinforces the image of Wilson as an unworldly valetudinarian. It is clear that he suffered significant, and by no means psychosomatic, illness throughout his life, and that his digestive ailments and series of small but successively disabling strokes did occasionally affect his judgement and ability to function on occasions. Equally, it is clear that specific emotional crises – notably the death of his first wife and engagement to his second – coincided with and in some way coloured his reaction to major events: as Europe slid into the war that now seems to define Wilson's political life, Ellen Axson Wilson was dying of Bright's disease; bracketing the critical period that saw the sinking of the *Falaba*, the *Lusitania* and the *Arabic* and the loss of 177 American lives to German torpedoes was Wilson's courtship of and eventual acceptance by Edith Bolling Galt. Though Wilson had a remarkable ability when required to bleach his public presentation of any purely private emotion – it was a more reticent time, in any case – there can be no doubt that these events changed his behaviour at the time.

However, as with any easy generalisation about Wilson, his 'obsession' with health is a backwards extrapolation from the knowledge that he suffered from several real ailments as well as imaginary ones, and to that extent is more apparent than actual. His health problems in young manhood may point to episodes of nervous prostration or to an early onset of hypertension, and the professorial or clerical figure Wilson cut in later years, with prominent false teeth and small eyeglasses did not suggest a man of action. On the other hand, Wilson was an enthusiastic baseball fan who had played centre field while at Davidson College in North Carolina and helped manage the varsity team at Princeton, though he was unable to win a playing place there. He became the first president officially to throw out the first ball at the World Series. The Wilsons had taken walking and cycling holidays in the Lake District and when the presidency restricted his physical freedom, he became an enthusiastic, if high-handicap, golfer; there is even a story that Secret Service agents painted some of his golf balls black so that he could play in snow in the White House grounds. Wilson may even have been addicted to exercise, a condition which affects many fit men and women who are subsequently pushed into sedentary lifestyles. When he was unable to take brisk walks, Wilson seems to have suffered non-specific ailments. In Paris, when he was locked in long and arduous negotiation over the shape and direction of the post-war world, his doctor and fellow-delegates forced him to exercise in front of an open window merely in order to get back some natural colour and appearance of vitality. He enjoyed fast cars, particularly convertibles, and liked the company of women; his libido seems to have been perfectly normal – he and Ellen Wilson had three daughters in four years. Despite Freud's and Bullitt's attempt to construct an Oedipal pathology, there seems to have been little abnormal in Wilson's family relationships, though he did continue to depend to an unusual, if not aberrant, extent on the close loyalty of his wife, secretary and a few political friends rather an extended circle. Nothing that points to a weakly or unduly neurotic personality, and indeed Clemenceau compared him favourably in terms of determination and stubbornness to General Pershing, commander of the American forces in Europe. Perverse though it inevitably sounds, no one fought more fiercely for peace than Woodrow Wilson, abandoning

WILLIAM JENNINGS BRYAN (1860–1925)
Though twice defeated for the presidency, William Jennings Bryan remained an iconic figure within the Democratic Party and an orator whose appeal was more visceral and less intellectual than Wilson's. Bryan's instinctive populism led him to be dubbed 'the Great Commoner' and he had his finest political moment with the famous 'Cross of Gold' speech at the 1896 Democratic National Convention in which he attacked the gold standard as an instrument of East Coast plutocracy.

Though his stance was effectively pacifist – leading to his resignation when Wilson responded robustly after the *Lusitania* sinking – Bryan did enlist during the 1898 Spanish-American war, though he did not see actual combat. He stood again for the presidency in 1900, and is believed to be the model for the Cowardly Lion in L Frank Baum's *The Wonderful Wizard of Oz.*

After defeat in the polls by William McKinley, Bryan became a tireless lecturer on the Chatauqua adult education circuit, mostly speaking on religious issues, promulgating the ideas of the Social Gospel and advocating peace. Such was his influence within the Democratic Party and in the agrarian Midwest that Wilson appointed him Secretary of State in 1912. Like Theodore Roosevelt but in apparent opposition to his own anti-war stance, Bryan petitioned the President direct to be conscripted after America did join the war, but he, too, was turned down.

In later years, he became active in Prohibition and temperance politics and waged a fierce campaign against Darwinist ideas. In the last weeks of his life, he argued the case for what would become known as creationism in the famous Scopes trial in Tennessee, where his antagonist was the very distinguished Clarence Darrow. Bryan seemed to collude in a directed verdict of guilty against the state of Tennessee, where the teaching of evolutionary theory had been forbidden, but his hope that the result might be over-ruled in a higher court was disappointed. Though his oratory was still powerful, Bryan's views seemed, in 1925, to be out of keeping with the spirit of the times. He died in his sleep just a few days after the Scopes trial ended.

his principle of 'peace without victory' almost as soon as the US entered the war, leaving its prosecution entirely to the generals (a situation unique in modern American history), and conducting his foreign policy with a belligerence that puzzled his future associates in battle (Britain and France were never formal US allies, as in the Second World War) and so alarmed the near-pacifist William Jennings Bryan that he resigned as Secretary of State.

It is striking how often in his speeches of the time, the great prophet of peace spoke of war, and of winning. Other aspects of his public presentation merit a second look, as well. Looked at more closely, Wilson's language does not so much reflect an obsessive concern with physical health as a metaphor for social wellness as a tendency – and this is a powerful clue to his political philosophy – to see all social processes as in some way organic and evolutionary rather than absolute and fixed. Physical health, disease, cure, morbidity were only sub-sets – and relatively minor ones – of a rhetorical apparatus that saw all measures as having the equivalent of life: being born (hence the grim appropriateness of Bailey's image of a 'Supreme Infanticide', the infant League smothered in its crib), growth, maturity, strength, wisdom, gradual or more sudden senescence. The 'body politic' had a near-literal significance for Wilson.

Other aspects of Wilson's reputation are less contentious or less easily warped. It is widely accepted that he was America's most academic – if not necessarily her most brilliant – leader, but it is important to understand that Wilson's contribution to academia was largely administrative rather than intellectual. His books are mostly plain and empirical, rather than flights of speculation. If he is commonly thought to be an idealist, that is because he had an uncommon brilliance with words, a rhetorician of rare skill, rather than because he subordinated 'realism' to ideals. A recent commentator opens his account 'Woodrow Wilson was a man of words', but is obliged to follow up with 'His actions weren't insignificant', in which the double negative is a fudge: the implication is that, as H W Brands makes clear in the opening line of his study, 'The Word' was paramount.[4]

There is a clue in this, which few historians seem willing to take up. Wilson seems complex, perhaps contradictory, psychologically volatile, arguably inconsistent in his opinions and positions largely because we have so much of his writing. *The Papers of Woodrow Wilson* constitute a remarkable 69 volumes, their compilation and editing overseen until his death by the doyen of Wilson studies, Arthur S Link.[5] Unlike other modern presidents and most modern politicians, Wilson composed his own speeches, usually bashed out on a hard-used portable typewriter – in an age when most secretarial work was undertaken by professional stenographers, Wilson was unusually proficient at shorthand and was using a Caligraph typewriter as early as 1883 – but the papers also include the myriad drafts, memos, position papers, letters and *aides-memoires* which catch him in the act of thinking. He was a writer before he was a politician and knew that the most effective way to test an idea is to put it into words rather than into action. His policy over the war, his dream of a League, his overlooked domestic reforms – Wilson intuited that his administration marked an effective end to the Progressive era in American politics and legislated accordingly when he had a Democratic Congress to legislate for him – were all subject to the same process of successive drafting, revision, abandonment and re-writing that a more literary writer might use. A Dutch historian, Jan Willem Schulte Nordholt characterised Wilson as a 'poet', which is both right and wrong.[6] His intellectual career was, indeed, a search for the perfect cadence, a fitness between message and form, but to see Wilson in this way is to see him from a European perspective. No American President – with the minor exception of Theodore Roosevelt – had left the United States during his administration. No-one subsequently ever stayed away so long. Even Franklin D Roosevelt's month-long journey to Yalta does not come close to the six months plus that Wilson stayed in Europe; between early December 1918 and early July 1919, he spent only two weeks in America, and then on unavoidable business. The situation might have sparked a small constitutional crisis. There was even a discussion as to whether Thomas R Marshall (how many non-specialists even remember the name of Wilson's vice-president?) should take over the Executive *pro tem*. Even more remarkably, though, when the president condemned by his opponents as an absentee or at best as a 'peripatetic' leader did return, he seemed no more minded to stay in Washington. The last, desperate campaign to bring the United States under the Treaty and into the League took him through the West and Midwest bringing him at last to Pueblo. To see him there is to see him in the only context he can be fully understood, not among the world's diplomats in Paris, but on the very American soil he had eschewed for half a year.

ooooo

Colorado's state motto is *Nil sine numine* – 'Nothing without Providence'. It is a sentiment that squares perfectly with Wilsonism, which in its essence and certainly in its expression was providential. There are three main strands to American foreign policy: the isolationism that defined it between Washington's so-called Farewell Address of 1796, with its warning against foreign entanglements, and the

Spanish-American conflict of 1898; the much later 'Realism' that insisted America accept its place in a fallen world, still morally superior, still with a mission to spread the gospels of peace, prosperity and democracy but unable to avoid contact with less privileged powers; though it drew and anticipated some elements from both, Wilson's philosophy was respectively less absolute and less fatalistic. As a politician, he was the creation and greatest expression of the so-called Progressive Era, but he was also a kind of Realist before the fact. Wilson's evolutionary instincts were rigorously applied, even to founding mythologies like the 'city that is set on a hill and cannot be hid' taken from St Matthew's Gospel, evoked in an extraordinary number of presidential inaugural addresses. In the words of historian Hugh Brogan: 'No doubt there has always been a tension in American minds between the idea that the city has been set upon a hill because it is already perfect and the idea that it has been set up in order to become perfect; in practice, the former notion prevails in times of insecurity ... while the other prevails in times of self-confidence.'[7]

Wilson's administration inherited the social confidence of progressivism, but ended in an atmosphere of changed realities and unexpected jitters. Though he embraced much of his old enemy Theodore Roosevelt's 'New Nationalism' during the war – 'the Colonel' had died suddenly and in his sleep on 6 January 1919, just as the Peace Conference was beginning – to his credit Wilson never fell back on the notion of America as a completed destiny.

He took a similar attitude to his religion, regarding the form and presentation of the gospel as almost more important than the content. As he himself observed in his journal, Wilson was capable of separating spiritual from intellectual satisfaction. He rationalised this as a refusal to allow his individual understanding to become the measure of all things – as one brand of Americanism saw the United States as setting the standard for all nations – but behind it was a pragmatic understanding, highly consistent with a political system that observed a strict separation of Church and State, that his religious observances were entire, aesthetic experiences determined by the form of individual acts of worship and the specific arts of suasion rather than by a single, unchanging Truth. Those who see Wilson as expounding and enacting a Christian gospel in world politics are as seriously misled as those who mistake the morning prayers that preceded business in the George W Bush administration as a fundamental component of policy and philosophy rather than an expression of the administration's presentational method.

... there is nothing so reassuring to men who are trying to express the public sentiment as getting into real personal contact with their fellow citizens.
WOODROW WILSON

In the opening moments of his address at the Civic Auditorium in Pueblo, Wilson tellingly commented on the *beautiful hall* in which he was speaking. *One of the advantages ... is that you are not too far away from me, because there is nothing so reassuring to men who are trying to express the public sentiment as getting into real personal contact with their fellow citizens.*[8] This immediately recalls the young Wilson who had spent hours in his father's pulpit practising public speaking, who felt instinctively easier addressing assemblies than individuals (psychohistorians have detected in this a symptom of emotional coldness and withdrawal) but the phrase *men who are trying to express the public sentiment* is fascinating; not 'shape' or 'influence', note, but 'express'.

This squares with a remarkable statement Wilson apparently made to an overseas visitor around the time the United States entered the First World War: *When I wish to know the true sentiment of my country, I lock myself in my study and sink into the depths of my consciousness as a citizen, and there I am sure to find it.*[9] The visitor came from Switzerland but unhappily was not Dr C G Jung, for here Wilson, so often the target of the Freudians, seems to be articulating something like the collective unconscious.

Whether such a thing existed in a democracy as young and volatile as America's, as chastened as America's in 1919, and in a part of America as far from Europe physically and temperamentally as Colorado is precisely the issue. Wilson, though no populist, had long understood that in a democracy policy *was* opinion, but expressed collectively rather than individually. While teaching at Wesleyan University, he had defined political leadership, with significant emphasis, as *interpretation.*[10] Wilson had an almost mystical belief, burnished by his admiration for Cobden, Bright and above all W E Gladstone, in the very British concept of 'going to the country', but in 1919 he must have been aware of how fractured that country was and how perturbed. A month before Wilson's visit to Pueblo, Senator Reed of Missouri described the national mood as one of 'shell shock'.[11] Given that America had not been invaded or bombarded during the conflict and that relatively few of her men had been lost in France, it is a diagnosis that requires some explanation.

Wars have a profound effect on national psychologies. The very fact of having turned so thoroughly away from many generations of isolationism as to become embroiled in a European conflict was a profound cultural shock, but one that manifested in unexpected ways. The journalist

Randolph Bourne, a waspish cripple with a scalpel-like intelligence, identified a kind of *trahison des clercs* among the American intelligentsia which threw itself – largely, Bourne and other pacifists remained resistant – behind the Allied cause and the war effort. Bourne's essay 'The War and the Intellectuals' published in *The Seven Arts* was a stinging rebuke. Though the war enriched America by making her a banker to the Allies – and particularly Britain – federal expenditure on the war exceeded the sum of all preceding expenditure since the ratification of the Constitution, a mind-boggling statistic and one that confirms Bourne's famous 'War is the Health of the State' slogan. The country was left in a curious position, under-governed at a quite fundamental level, but also subject to restrictions and controls that were profoundly un-American in spirit. The transport infrastructure had been nationalised to facilitate movement of troops and materiel. Legislation had been introduced that seemed to infringe freedom of speech – the veteran Socialist politician Eugene Debs was imprisoned for his opposition to the war – and in some cases enforced strict censorship. The Espionage Act of June 1917 and the Sedition Acts of 1918 were unprecedented since the days of the Revolution. The passing of the 18th Amendment to the Constitution in January 1919 led to a piece of enabling legislation later that year known as the Volstead Act which ushered in the Prohibition period, a curious episode in American life not so much because suspicion of alcohol was new – more than 30 states already practised restriction or were notionally 'dry' – but more because it was the Federal government that was imposing the restriction at a time when the President had been out of the country on what many saw as non-American business for six months.

Production of alcohol had already been significantly disrupted by the war, with the use of grains and other materials normally used for producing strong drink diverted into regular food use. Given that beer production was the fief of German-American families, perhaps distantly related to the U-boat commanders and crews who had taken American lives in the Atlantic, a further measure of boycott increased the pressure. The question of race and ethnicity was a profound one. 1919 saw a dramatic increase in racial violence, with more than 80 lynchings reported and the black nationalist Marcus Garvey pointing out that black regiments had taken the brunt of casualties in the war against the Kaiser, only to be slighted, abused and in extreme cases stoned and hanged on their return home. A Southerner, Wilson seemed ambivalent on the subject of race. As president of Princeton University, he had discouraged African-Americans even from applying for entry. As president of the country, he introduced segregation into federal employment – separate lunchrooms and other facilities – though he seemed also to be a meritocrat, making significant and unpopular appointments of black candidates to key jobs. He had been a fellow-student at Johns Hopkins University of Thomas Dixon, author of *The Clansman*, on which D W Griffith's notorious film *The Birth of a Nation* (1915) was based. Wilson's own words on the emergence of the Ku Klux Klan were captioned during the film, which Wilson showed regularly at the White House, allegedly declaring it to be *like writing history with lightning … all so terribly true*, though no one can ascertain whether he actually said this; he certainly disapproved of the later resurgence and violence of the Klan.[12]

A more insidious kind of racism had crept into America, stoked by fear of Bolshevism and a renewed outbreak of anarchist violence – bombs started turning up in packages to public officials in the spring of 1919 – but largely determined by industrial unrest as America gradually stood down her war economy and struggled with the demographic and employment disturbances brought about by demobilisation. Attorney-General A Mitchell Palmer – perhaps with political ambitions of his own – launched an increasingly paranoid campaign against any who seemed to run counter to '100 per cent Americanism'. Though less celebrated than the McCarthy witchhunts of the post-Second World War years, the 'Palmer raids', which led to the deportation of almost 1,000 suspect aliens – most of them demonstrably innocent of any nefarious intent – were a profound cultural shock and unleashed on the country a new Bureau of Investigation (forerunner to the FBI) and a new love-hate figure called J Edgar Hoover, who for the next half-century would define a particular brand of American paranoia and infringement of individual liberty and freedom of thought.

Wilson himself was not immune to the spirit of paranoia. When he travelled through the Midwest states, he must have been aware that substantial proportions of the audiences he addressed would have been of German ancestry, not as high as in the Great Lakes states and in the East, but these were lost to the Republicans anyway. In Colorado, unlike Nebraska or Wisconsin, where the proportion was about 40 per cent, the figure was just over one-fifth, with a further eighth of the population of Irish ancestry. Among these were the 'hyphenates' who Wilson – in a somewhat chilling anticipation of Adolf Hitler's rhetoric – accused of stabbing America in the back. Speaking of German-Americans and Irish-Americans in particular (Wilson did claim some Irish lineage when it suited him) he described the hyphen as a *serpent*, and suggested in

'HYPHENATE' AMERICANS

The suspect loyalty and political sympathies of so-called 'hyphenate' Americans – the term was actually first used by Theodore Roosevelt – was a major issue for Wilson and his administration between 1914 and 1917, and the 1916 Republican presidential candidate Charles Evans Hughes may have lost significant support when his concept of 'dominant Americanism' (i.e. loyalty to the country of adoption over that retained for the country of cultural origin) clashed with a rising tide of nativism.

The proportion of Americans of German extraction currently stands at somewhat under one-fifth. Specifically German settlement began as early as 1608, but in later years tended to concentrate in the Midwest and around the Great Lakes; Joseph Ruggles Wilson's birthplace of Steubenville in Jefferson County, Ohio, was named in honour of Baron Friedrich Wilhelm von Steuben, a Prussian who acted as Inspector General of the Continental Army during the War of Independence and subsequently wrote the basic drill manual for the American army. Between 1850 (immediately after a period of political unrest and revolutionary or nationalistic activity across Europe) and 1900, Germans were by far the largest cultural group emigrating to the US, some six million in number, and consequently many were still not fully assimilated by the time of the First World War. Some intellectuals, including the journalist H L Mencken and the Harvard applied psychologist Hugo Münsterberg (who died in 1916) came out in favour of Germany during the war, arguing that German social democracy was more highly developed. Herbert Hoover's German ancestry (originally Huber) perhaps lent extra urgency to his desire to provide aid after the armistice.

However, ordinary Germans were increasingly treated with suspicion, and many were coerced into buying war bonds to demonstrate loyalty. The Prohibition movement had an implicitly or sometimes openly anti-German dimension, since German-Americans dominated the brewing industry. Physical attacks and even a number of lynchings occurred, though for the most part systematic hostility was expressed in the form of (constitutionally illegal) restrictions on speaking German in public and the teaching of the language. Religious observance in German was less frequently attacked, but German music was largely excluded from concert programmes and German-born conductors ostracised.

Systematic wartime propaganda did much to marginalise the German-American community but relations normalised relatively quickly after the war.

Pueblo that *any man who carries a hyphen about with him carries a dagger that he is ready to plunge into the vitals of this Republic whenever he gets ready. If I can catch any man with a hyphen in this great contest I will know that I have got an enemy of the Republic.* This chimes rather strangely – or at best ironically – with his opening remarks on *the homogeneity of this great people to whom we belong. They come from many stocks but they are all of one kind. They come from many originals, but they are shot through with the same principles and desire the same righteous and honest things.*[13] This is wishful at best, for it was precisely the absence of homogeneity and accord that had kept Wilson out of the war until 1917 and one of the main issues on which he fought his 1916 presidential opponent Charles Evans Hughes, who declared that 'dominant Americanism' permitted, or even enjoined, foreign-born Americans and those not yet culturally assimilated to be whole-hearted in their patriotism when the need arose. Bourne, as ever, was among the first to recognise – this in the summer of 1916 – that 'No reverbatory effect of the great war [reverbatory because the US was not yet a combatant] has caused American public opinion more solicitude than the failure of the "melting-pot".'[14]

Creating a relative consensus in favour of war against Germany was the result of a massive public relations exercise and a propaganda machine that continued spinning wildly at war's end, fuelling the 'Red Scare' and in the process sowing the seeds of the Cold War. In late 1914 and for all his desire to exert an influence in Europe, his concerns were almost entirely internal rather than external. The British Ambassador to the US, Sir Cecil Spring-Rice, paraphrased the President's concerns in a memo of January 1918 to the Foreign Secretary A J Balfour: 'There was imminent danger of civil discord, the speaking tour in defence of the League. Wilson had returned from Europe physically depleted. The minor strokes that had afflicted him since 1896 had done lasting harm. The unending round of negotiation and discussion in Paris – with less time than usual for the walks, cycle runs and rounds of golf Wilson depended on to recover his energies – had led to a viral infection which laid him low for a time at Paris in April 1919 (and in the view of at least one recent historian significantly weakened his resolve as well as his constitution).

Japan and Australia had imposed travel restrictions during the epidemic and had saved significant number of lives as a result. There were some local initiatives in America (including wearing masks on streetcars in some cities) but federal regulation did not stretch to more comprehensive regulation, a perverse example of under-government, but by June 1919 the epidemic had run its course in the US. Edith Wilson and Dr Grayson were more concerned with the summer heat and the rigours of making a projected 40 speeches in 25 days. Leaving aside its medical unwisdom, Wilson's speaking tour was a pointless gesture. In reality, ratification of the Treaty and League depended on the 'bungalow minds' in the Senate – his contempt was ill-concealed – and not on the American people, but Wilson, politically weakened by substantial Republican victories in Congress in the November 1918 elections, was also aware that 1920 was a presidential election year and that a third term – still constitutionally possible – could not be ruled out. Wilson stoutly denied having any such thought, declaring it shameful and the purpose of his tour non-partisan, but he refused to declare that he would not seek re-election.

The Republican Party, too, was aware that a presidential election was looming and was determined that Wilson's triumph should be sharply limited. That is not to say that the Grand Old Party was of a mind on the question of the Treaty. Only the so-called 'Irreconcilables' – otherwise 'Bitter-enders' or 'The Battalion of Death' – were implacably opposed to it in any shape or form. More dangerous were the 'Strong Reservationists', headed by Senator Henry Cabot Lodge, who proposed such amendments to the Treaty as to render null most of Wilson's main points and principles. Sitting between these two factions were the 'Mild Reservationists', whose proposed changes were not sufficiently radical to hole the Treaty below the waterline.

In July 1919, as chair of the Senate Foreign Relations Committee, Lodge read – aloud, and often to an empty committee room; even his clerk disappeared for comfort breaks – all 264 pages of the Treaty. Then the public hearings began, calling as many as 60 highly suspect or at least questionably partisan witnesses mostly to complain of ethnic or national inequities in the treaty. The body of testimony amounted to nearly 1,300 pages. It reads like an absurdist filibuster, an attempt to swamp Wilson's faith in 'the Word' with words. Nonetheless, he believed, with some justification, that he had the American people on his side.

Wilson's chief avowed reason for going ahead, despite serious gastro-intestinal problems and alarming headaches, was that it would be shaming to show weakness when so many *boys* – he still spoke like the university baseball coach he had once been – had suffered worse and died in France without complaint. He was not so blinded with sentiment, though, as to attempt to preach to either the converted or the unconvertible. The South was his stronghold, and could be counted on. The East could be counted on to say no. On the other hand, the West had handed him a mandate – whether for peace or victory was not entirely clear – in 1916 but had since fallen back into Republican arms. The Midwest was quietly hostile or at best sceptical. These were the obvious battlegrounds.

On the outward journey, Wilson was met initially with diffidence. So far from the sea, so predominantly agrarian in culture and politics, perhaps not yet ready to lay down the hyphen that qualified their Americanism, they were wary of his vision, though not openly hostile to it. Unexpectedly – to everyone except Wilson – the West rose to him with warmth and in some cases passion. Even in Idaho he received a rapturous reception. This was the home state of the most hard-boiled of all the Irreconcilables. Senator William E Borah, portrayed in cartoons either as the 'Idaho lion' or else as a human phonograph bellowing anti-League, anti-Democratic, anti-Wilson statements of dubious propriety, had made it clear that even if Jesus Christ himself came to Des Moines to plead the cause of the League, he would not be listened to. Borah was wrong. Wilson was vindicated.

The recognition proved fatal to him. Mrs Wilson and Dr Grayson tried to persuade him to cancel his remaining appearances and return to Washington for some much-needed rest, but the president was convinced that he had built up an irresistible popular momentum. Mass communications had not yet reached a stage where an address in one state would simultaneously be broadcast or rapidly reported in another, but telegraph and telephone did mean that his words were published ahead of his arrival. Besides, Wilson was too shrewd a politician to think that a single speech would fit every setting, and was too vain a writer to repeat himself. With no speech-writer to impose a superficial consistency of tone, he continued to vary his great theme, and was often seen on the presidential train bent over his typewriter rattling out the next speech only an hour or so after delivering the peroration to the last.

The sequence of speeches suggests a rising cadence of emotion, but Wilson's growing fervour was at odds with his declining health. In Pueblo, strikingly pale, he battled a fierce headache and was seen to dab his lips several times as he read his text. Much of it was intended to reassure Americans that accepting the Treaty and joining the League would in no way disadvantage the United States in the world community, and to set at rest German-American minds that the six proposed votes of the United Kingdom and her Dominions were in the assembly only and not in council and would not in any case – here a swell of forthright Americanism – add up to the one vote of the United States (strictly, it was three if one included protectorates like Panama and Puerto Rico).

He moved on to Article X of the League Covenant, that the members would severally and together guarantee the self-determination of any sovereign power against foreign aggression – not internal disturbance – and that Council would proceed to *advise* only – *I do not know any other meaning for the word 'advise' other than 'advise'* – on appropriate action. This to still Borah's insistence and that of others that to commit America to the League was both treacherous and treasonable and a wanton surrender of American sovereignty.

The tone was factual, reassuring, almost academic, a professor of jurisprudence clarifying points of law rather than a politician winning hearts and minds. Wilson went on to make clear that even as he held certain principles sacred he was not beyond compromise, reminding his audience that he had met with Lodge and other opponents, heard their reservations, absorbed their recommendations, taken them to France and seen them adopted.

Then, though, the speech took a new turn. Wilson invoked the mothers who have clutched his hand and wept on it, crying 'God bless you, Mr President!' But why does he deserve their blessing? Because their dead sons perished for a cause that transcends national objectives and war aims. In dying, they *saved the liberty of the world*. He called them *crusaders*, a measure of how far acceptable rhetoric has changed in 90 years, and then he played his trump card. *There seem to me to stand between us and the rejection of qualification of this treaty the serried ranks of those boys in khaki, not only those boys who came home, but those dear ghosts that still deploy upon the fields of France.*

There seem to me to stand between us and the rejection or qualification of this treaty the serried ranks of those boys in khaki, not only these boys who came home, but those dear ghosts that still deploy upon the fields of France.

WOODROW WILSON, SPEECH IN PUEBLO, COLORADO, 25 SEPTEMBER 1919

At this point, Wilson broke down and was not able to continue for some moments. His concluding words had the air of a benediction. Once the mists of contention cleared away, the American people would, Wilson believed, reaffirm their commitment to the truth of justice, liberty and peace, a truth that *is going to lead us, and through us the world, out into pastures of quietness and peace such as the world never dreamed of before*. Wilson himself enjoyed no peace that night. Plagued with insomnia, Wilson suffered another severe headache. The following morning, the left side of his face drooped stiffly and his speech was slurred. Edith and Grayson overruled his protests and hurried the President back to Washington. This time, there was to be no glimpse of him bashing out another moving defence of the Treaty. The blinds of his carriage were down. On 2 October, back at the White House, he suffered a disabling stroke. Woodrow Wilson lived for another four and a half years. He even outlived his successor in the White House, but he was never again a well man and the reins of government effectively fell from his hands. The one-time defender of cabinet government never again chaired a full meeting of his own, though a change in perception of his own role had a greater hand in that than declining health. Though Grayson had admitted to the press that the President had suffered a complete nervous collapse in Pueblo – an admission almost unthinkable in present-day politics, though the fact could hardly be concealed for long – the extent of his illness was concealed from the public for the rest of his administration. Those close to Wilson found him lachrymose and easily disturbed; political allies and opponents – the former to their dismay, the latter to considerable satisfaction – found him unmoveable.

This is to anticipate the story substantially, but events moved swiftly in Wilson's absence, and with a seeming perversity. Senator Gilbert M Hitchcock was the acting minority leader in the Senate. He came to Wilson's sickroom to plead with the President to accept some of the Reservationists' demands. Though frail, Wilson would not budge and his obduracy had the effect of either re-uniting the Republican ranks or rendering their differences irrelevant. The details of and the reasons for the successive votes taken in the Senate on 19 November 1919 are matter for a later chapter, but Wilson's inability to compromise turned him indeed into the 'Supreme Infanticide'.

The USA would make a separate peace with Germany

and would never join the League of Nations, a situation that can only be described as '*Hamlet*-without-the-Prince', and in every possible sense of that cliché. Its history was marked by fudge and inaction, high-sounding rhetoric unmatched by deed, its would-be hero philosophically detached from a world it was destined to inherit, the ensuing bloodbath all the greater for the failure to resolve a past violence decisively and with principle. Just as everyone knows that 'Versailles' – usually uttered with a hiss – was 'responsible' for the Second World War, everyone knows that Woodrow Wilson was its architect and that of the doomed League of Nations. How he came to be, how his principles and his actions affected not just the wider world but also America herself, and how seeming contradiction crept into the political career of a man defined as the model of moral rectitude is a much larger story. And it is one that has to be told not just through the lens of large economic and political and cultural forces but, almost uniquely in the politics of the time, through the life and personality, learning and career of one man who remade American politics even as he led it and who shaped the future course of the world even as he lost final grip on his own vision for it.

President Wilson throws out the first ball of the baseball season in 1916. His wife Edith is on the left.

I

The Life and the Land

1
Exegetical and *evangelical*

Britain's wartime ambassador to the US, Sir Cecil Spring-Rice, described Woodrow Wilson as a 'mysterious personage'.[1] There is a potentially straightforward explanation for the comment, for Spring-Rice was a friend of Wilson's enemy, former president Theodore Roosevelt (or 'TR' as he was known), who he considered childlike but engaging, a verdict that considerably underestimated TR's abilities. Additionally, the comment might be considered the pot calling the kettle black for Spring-Rice himself was often acutely paranoid – believing himself beset with German spies – and more generally inclined to adopt the manners of a viceroy rather than a diplomat. In reality, he and Wilson had much in common, in background and temperament if not politically.

Wartime service took a heavy toll on both men's questionable health. Spring-Rice was abruptly recalled to the UK in February 1918 and died suddenly in Ottawa on the journey home. Neither man was inclined to delegate and Spring-Rice bridled furiously when Lord Northcliffe was appointed War Commissioner in Washington, ostensibly to lighten his load but perhaps also to mitigate an uneasy relationship with the

White House. Both men were at bottom writers first and politicians largely as a result of their literary ambitions: Spring-Rice's single greatest legacy is the words to the hymn 'I Vow To Thee My Country', a lyric poem which also reflects their common tendency to conflate spirituality and nationalism.

If Woodrow Wilson was mysterious, much of the mystery – or at least many of his more enigmatic attitudes and habits of mind – can be traced back to his childhood and background. Even the matter of his given name throws up one of those small unanswered questions that have exercised biographers of the freudianising sort who consider that all adult actions and opinions can be explained by events in early life. Until the age of 23, when he graduated from Princeton University, he had been Thomas W Wilson, or Tommy at home, but when he returned to his *alma mater* as its president a decade later, his first significant political appointment, he had dropped the Thomas, apparently at his mother's most particular request. There is a single reference to this in a letter, no explanation offered as to why the request should have been made, or whether it was a sudden change of mind or a long-standing dissatisfaction with his christened name.

Janet Wilson had been a Woodrow and perhaps simply wanted to honour the name. The daughter and sister of Presbyterian ministers, she was of Scottish stock, though born just over the English border in Carlisle. Unlike her future husband, she was an immigrant to the US, and according to family story only narrowly survived the voyage when a freak wave swept across the deck of the ship that carried the family over. The hypochondriac tendency she seems to have passed on to her son may well have begun or been exaggerated by the trauma, though such mishaps were by no means uncommon on the still-perilous transatlantic voyage. The Wilsons were in

America already, Scots-Irish settlers from Strabane, County Tyrone in Ulster. The future president's father, the Reverend Dr Joseph Ruggles Wilson grew up in Steubenville, Ohio, on the eastern border of the state. The family was Republican, and Dr Wilson's grandfather was publisher of an abolitionist newspaper, the pre-state Northwest Territory having forbidden slavery by ordinance in 1787.

Though his roots were in the Midwest, and he was intellectually shaped in the North, Woodrow Wilson was a son of the South. In novelist and alternative historian Harry Turtledove's *Timeline-191* sequence, Wilson is the tenth president of the Confederate States of America, elected on a Whig ticket, and drawn into a wartime alliance with Britain and France against Theodore Roosevelt's pro-German United States of America. Though a work of fantasy and therefore necessarily counter-factual, Turtledove's *'Great War'* trilogy is by no means counter-intuitive. Dr Wilson served as a chaplain with the Confederate Army during the Civil War, when his church was used as a hospital for wounded Confederate soldiers and also as a holding area for Union prisoners. He was a founding member in 1861 of the Presbyterian Church of the United States (PCUS), a breakaway Southern splinter that emphasised conservative and scholarly values, as well as a strict application of the Calvinist confession. Despite his abolitionist background, Dr Wilson quickly became an apologist for the institution of slavery, publishing – with a nice show of reluctance – a sermon on the 'Mutual Relations of Masters and Slaves As Taught in the Bible'.[2] Dr Wilson seems to have treated his own slaves with a condescending benevolence that he certainly passed on to his son. His establishment of a black Sunday school in Georgia is striking similar to Woodrow Wilson's equal-but-separate approach to federal employment during his first administration.

Joseph Wilson was educated at Steubenville Academy and at Jefferson College, Pennsylvania. He received his vocational training at Western Theological and Princeton Theological Seminaries, and was ordained in 1849, the same year he met and married Jessie Woodrow; he was 27, Jessie was four years younger, and a student. Their first child, Marion Morton Wilson (later Kennedy) was born a year later. The couple moved South in 1851, and two years later a second daughter, Annie Josephine Wilson (later Howe) added to the family. Dr Wilson worked as locum minister to a number of congregations and as a college teacher until he was called as pastor to the First Presbyterian Church in Staunton, a small town in the Shenandoah Valley.

Ohio is one of two states to claim the title of 'Mother of Presidents'. The other, more obviously, given the early history of the Republic, is Virginia, and on 28 December 1856 (at two minutes past midnight, so strictly the 29th, though the family celebrated the earlier day), Thomas Woodrow Wilson became the eighth – and so far the last – future president to be born in the commonwealth. Tommy Wilson was still only two years old when his father was called to Augusta, Georgia, so he can have remembered almost nothing about his birthplace. In later life, he claimed that his first conscious memory was of hearing that Abraham Lincoln had been elected president and that there would be war; the election took place in early November 1860, just weeks before Joseph Wilson delivered that sermon on 'Masters and Slaves' which his parishioners persuaded him to publish. When he rose to the pulpit on 6 January 1861, the family's future home state of South Carolina had already seceded from the Union.

Others rapidly followed, with Georgia declaring secession on 18 January. Three weeks later, the Confederate States of America were formed. Lincoln was smuggled into Washington DC for his inauguration, following an assassination attempt in Baltimore.

Though Georgia saw little military action until 1863, and Augusta remained largely unscathed, the state's transport and economic infrastructure were devastated by more than 500 battles and smaller engagements during the final two years of the conflict. Sherman's March to the Sea is the stuff of bloody legend. At Andersonville, south of Macon in central Georgia, 13,000 Union prisoners of war died of hunger, disease and ritual punishments, or were shot when they strayed across the 'deadline'. Tommy Wilson could not have been protected from all these horrors and it seems from the future president's own later testimony that his father considered it a bounden duty to explain all matters to his son, however complex or harsh. Wilson's strongest memory of the war was of gazing up into the face of the Southern hero General Robert E Lee.

In later years, Wilson considered himself an American rather than a Southerner. In later years, the adept and subtle debate presented a historical and moral rationalisation whereby the South had fought in an honourable cause and for a profound constitutional right, but that the North's victory had been the only acceptable outcome. Wilson often presented himself as a rebel from his own class and region. He retained 'Southern' manners – if not the Southern drawl Harold Nicholson (and almost no others) claimed to hear in Paris – and was courteous and charming to ladies. Perhaps more than charming; there were rumours of inappropriate friendships and one apparent affair, though otherwise the Wilson administration was notably free of sexual scandal; this in contrast to that of his successor Warren G Harding, target of the first kiss-and-tell book, Nan Britton's *The President's Daughter* in which she claimed to have had sex with the president in a walk-in White House closet and borne his illegitimate child; and in contrast to both Abraham Lincoln and his predecessor James Buchanan, both of whom were believed by enemies to be gay, in the bachelor Buchanan's case convincingly so. Other Southern attitudes settled deep in Wilson. With a 47 per cent African-American population, Georgia inevitably suffered some of the worst excesses associated with post-Civil War Reconstruction, including an enforced Black suffrage and the descent on the state of opportunistic Ohio and other Northern 'carpetbaggers'. Wilson apparently endorsed *The Birth of a Nation* as an accurate portrayal of the period; unfortunately, the film also acted as a catalyst for the formation of a second Klan, the original movement having petered out after Reconstruction. Georgia was the last state to re-enter the Union – in 1870 – and has returned Democrat governors ever since, at least until the shock result of 2003. Woodrow Wilson's commitment to the Democratic Party was instinctive, unswerving and lifelong.

In 1867, the Wilsons had a fourth child and second son. This must have put further pressure on the family economy. Though Wilson grew up in a series of roomy manses, a Presbyterian minister's stipend was small and would only have been supplemented by Dr Wilson's teaching. On one famous occasion, he was stopped by a parishioner who pointed out – with what level of good humour or sour disapproval can't be judged – that the minister's horse looked better groomed than he did. Dr Wilson crisply replied that while he looked after his horse, it was the parish that looked after him. It is a much-quoted anecdote, and suggests a quick-witted and pawky personality, somewhat removed from the God-like and domineering superego figure of the Freudian biographers. With two older sisters and with Joseph Ruggles Wilson II (who became a journalist in adult life) more than a decade younger, Tommy Wilson was understandably the main focus of his family's ambitions and expectations. Jessie Wilson coached him in the social proprieties, and may have fussed over his health; while the boy's formal education was entrusted to private tutors and small schools, Dr Wilson filled his head with facts; one can readily imagine Marion and Annie marvelling over their little brother's cleverness. There is nothing in Wilson's life to suggest that his childhood was not happy and well-supported. The idea of him as a *de facto* only child is not convincing. All through his life, he depended on the understanding (and to some degree praise) of a small circle of intimates. This is not merely psychological finessing: Wilson's conduct of policy and his approach to both war and peace while president strongly reflects a dependence on sympathetic intimates.

Dr Wilson died in his son's house in 1903 – Jessie had passed away 15 years earlier – and seems in his later years to have devoted himself to furthering the boy's career. When Wilson published his first book, the dedication was to *the patient guide of [my] youth, the gracious companion of [my] manhood, [my] best instructor and most lenient critic.* 'Patient', 'gracious' and 'lenient' do not sound like *pro forma* compliments. That Woodrow Wilson might one day write a book at all would have seemed improbable in his early teens. For reasons that are not satisfactorily explained – though may be due to a form of dyslexia – Wilson did not learn to read until he was 12. Even in later life, and in sharp contrast to a document-devouring modern executive like John F Kennedy, he remained a slow reader and a writer who favoured simple and straightforward exegesis: hence, perhaps, the form if not the substance of his Fourteen Points. Typically, though, Wilson taught himself a form of shorthand, to which he applied himself with the kind of 'industry' his father admired.

Interestingly, there seems to have been no point at which Wilson considered following his father (or his maternal grandfather and uncles) into the ministry. In his 'dream' life, he imagined being an admiral or a senator. His religious beliefs were strong, but also carefully compartmentalised. The image of Wilson at the Peace Conference as a Christian crusader is seriously misleading. As more than one commentator has noted, he had the ability to keep the intellectual and fiducial aspects of his mind entirely separate, writing in his journal in 1889 that he found himself *capable ... of being satisfied spiritually without being satisfied intellectually*.[3] 'Satisfied' may also be a significant choice of word.

At the end of the Civil War, Dr Wilson was appointed stated clerk of the PCUS, an office he held for more than 30 years; in 1879, he acted as Moderator, an honorary but important post. In 1870, he was appointed professor at a Presbyterian seminary in Columbia, South Carolina, but the school was on a precarious financial footing and riven with the doctrinal differences that ran through American Presbyterianism at the time. Four years later, the school was obliged to close for a time, and Dr Wilson was called as minister to Wilmington in the same state. At this point, Tommy Wilson was completing his freshman year at Davidson College (his father was a trustee), a short distance from Columbia, and developing his own oratorical skills as an active member of the debating society and – surprisingly for such a slow learner – developing a passion for literature: on or around 4 July the following year, he wrote to a friend *I like nothing so well as writing and talking.*[4]

By then, though, opportunities for the latter, certainly with men of his own age, had dried up, leaving considerably more time for the former; Wilson did not return to Davidson for his sophomore year, either because of a breakdown in health (nervous strain or an early appearance of hypertension) or else equally probably because Dr Wilson could no longer afford his fees. Wilson spent almost a year in the family home, but in September 1875 he made a decisive and more than symbolic journey from South to North. Though it was not yet a permanent move away – that happened in 1883, when he went to Baltimore – it affected his outlook and shaped his early career profoundly.

I like nothing so well as writing and talking.
WOODROW WILSON

Joseph Wilson had studied at Princeton Theological Seminary and knew the principal of the College of New Jersey, later to be Princeton University. The Reverend James McCosh, who had taught moral philosophy in Belfast, was a personal friend and while on a fund-raising and talent-scouting trip to the South, visited the Wilsons and, obviously impressed by the older son's seriousness and application, offered him a place. Given his initiatives as Princeton president a quarter of a century later, it's not surprising to find Wilson initially less than enchanted with the place. At the height of his reforms, the *New York Post* sarcastically, but perhaps also admiringly, noted that Wilson had destroyed 'the most agreeable and aristocratic country club in America by transforming it into an institution of learning'.[5] Wilson did join one of the dining clubs at the college, a relatively new group called the Alligators (presumably with a substantial Southern membership;

the College was popular with Southerners), and quickly threw himself into the American Whig Society and other discussion groups. He also began writing for *The Princetonian*, which he later edited. He found class work tedious, though, and complained that the college put more emphasis on dry learning than on dialectic, oratory and the arts of persuasion. If the pulpit was not beckoning, public office already appears to have been. The dream was already far in advance of the reality: he had visiting cards printed that read 'Thomas Woodrow Wilson, senator from Virginia'.

What is the object of oratory? Its object is persuasion and conviction – the control of other minds by a strange personal influence and power.

WOODROW WILSON EDITORIAL IN THE PRINCETONIAN, 7 JUNE 1877.[6]

Nothing could have galvanised the young politician in Wilson more than the presidential election of 1876, one of the most controversial in US history. The centennial election was not only closely contested, its result was disputed, and the compromise that resolved it made a major impact on the South. The two main contenders were the reformist Republican Rutherford B Hayes from Ohio and opposing him Samuel J Tilden, a Bourbon (that is, a classical liberal and conservative) Democrat from New York who stood strong against the corruption of the outgoing administration of Ulysses S Grant. Among the other parties were a nativist 'American' party, a Prohibitionist lobby, and an inflationary 'Greenback' party of mostly agricultural interests who spoke to a need for mass production of paper money to energise the economy.

The popular ballot gave 4,288,546 to Tilden and 4,034,311 to Hayes, but there were serious charges of misconduct and fraud in three Southern states, Louisiana, Wilson's home state of South Carolina, and – in anticipation of the even more closely run and controversial presidential election of 2000 – Florida. The electors who cast the actual votes for president were inconsistently selected, ballot papers printed with symbols for the benefit of illiterate voters were deliberately confusing (with Abe Lincoln's face used for the Democratic ballot) and there were charges of intimidation and violence against known Republicans. In addition to the 19 electoral votes commanded by Louisiana, South Carolina and Florida, an Oregon elector was challenged. A commission of inquiry was set up to consider the results and decided to award all the disputed votes to Hayes. In addition, Colorado, where Wilson gave his climactic speech in support of the League of Nations 43 years later, had only just been admitted to the Union as a state and was participating in its first presidential election; its vote went to Hayes, too. The final tally of electors was 185 to 184 in the Republicans' favour.

Wilson must have watched this unfold with fascination. He seems to have observed campus squabbles and fisticuffs between one side and the other with fascinated horror. When the ballots had been re-examined in South Carolina, it was decided that Hayes had won the state by just 889 votes, the second narrowest (after Florida's 537 in 2000) in US history. Wilson had been an enthusiastic Tilden supporter, but, somewhat like his heart-versus-head reaction to the outcome of the Civil War, was unconvinced that the Democratic constituency and its representatives were in any way fit for or worthy of office. He would also have been aware that the trade-off for Hayes's victory was a withdrawal of Federal troops from the South, marking an effective end to the period of enforced Reconstruction, and every Southerner would have welcomed that. Almost as important though, the election and its aftermath fuelled what became Wilson's lifelong interest in the nature of American government.

Intriguingly, when Wilson wrote to his wife just before making his inaugural address at Princeton, he likened himself to a prime minister rather than a president.[7] His first political models and guiding philosophies were British. He profoundly admired Walter Bagehot, author of *The English Constitution* (1867), and acquired something of Bagehot's easy style and ability to deliver a stinging generality with wit and elegance. In his chapter on 'The Cabinet', Bagehot had said that 'the great qualities, the imperious will, the rapid energy, the eager nature fit for a great crisis are not required – are impediments – in common times' and that statement almost perfectly sums up Wilson's own political nature and wartime administration.[8] At the time, though, he was more interested in what Bagehot said about cabinet government and attempted to adapt it to an American context. Though he also admired native American heroes like George Washington, about whom he wrote a book in 1896, Wilson deeply admired the oratory of Edmund Burke, whose conservative interpretation of liberty instinctively appealed, and idolised the great Liberal statesman W E Gladstone. Bagehot's observation, of Sir Robert Peel, in his *Biographical Studies*, that 'a constitutional statesman is in general a man of common opinion and uncommon abilities' would surely have been supported by Wilson.[9] This goes to the heart of Wilson's unsentimental view of politics-as-interpretation, the ability by exceptional rhetorical talent to harness and shape by debate the otherwise flabby, self-serving and unpredictable will-of-the-people. As college president and as national president, as fiscal reformer and as the would-be architect of world peace, this was the guiding principle of Woodrow Wilson's career.

He was beginning to be known. An article on 'Cabinet Government in the United States', very much influenced by Bagehot, appeared in *International Review* a matter of weeks after Wilson graduated in the summer of 1879. In it, he proposed a more balanced relationship between executive and legislative branches of government. The Reconstruction period, in contrast to the Civil War itself, when Abraham Lincoln acquired some of the authority of a dictator, was one in which the power of Congress was greatly increased. Lincoln's successor Andrew Johnson was tried and impeached for removing Secretary of War Edwin Stanton from office. The reprisal was swift; a *Harper's Weekly* cartoon shows Stanton aiming a cannon at the hapless president – the cannon is inscribed 'CONGRESS'. As a Southern Democrat, Wilson would have had a natural suspicion of excessive congressional power, but he was already in transition, politically and intellectually, and his main point of concern at this period seems to have been the lack of opportunity for men of real talent in American politics; or with a different emphasis, the lack of genuinely talented individuals to take the place of the spoilsmen and time-servers who ran Washington. 'Transcendent influence' was his ideal, but the two decades after the Civil War were darksome times for American politics and his vision would have to wait.

His own immediate future, as opposed to his long-term commitment to public service on the largest scale, was not yet settled. Throughout his life, and even after the catastrophic stroke of 1919, Wilson believed that it was his destiny to write what would amount to the *Principia Mathematica* of political theory, an inductive study of democratic government that he himself saw as the potential successor to Montesquieu's *L'Esprit des lois*. Though he himself recognised that his preferred route to political office was through writing, it may be that pressure from his father persuaded him not just to write about 'laws' in the abstract, but to practise law. It was not, as he acknowledged, to be the happiest decision of his life.

In the autumn of 1879, Wilson began his course at the Virginia Law School. It is again not clear whether his father's financial difficulties, his own apparent dislike of the work, or a genuine decline in health led him to leave the following December. However, it is clear that whatever the first cause, and despite Dr Wilson's anxiety that he should see through his training, Jessie Wilson was equally insistent that he should return to the family home and to her care. Wilson continued his studies there, and used his father's pulpit to practise the oratorical skills he would require in the courtroom. In May 1882, he moved to Atlanta as partner of a friend from law school Edward A Renick. Five months later, he passed the bar with an impressive performance before the redoubtable Judge George Hillyer, who had seen service with the Confederate Army in the Gettysburg campaign and who subsequently held office as Atlanta mayor and state senator. Wilson found the practice of the law as dull as he had its study and the firm of Renick & Wilson struggled to find clients, the partners' idealism often at odds with forensic practicality. He told his friend Robert Bridges *I cannot breathe freely nor smile readily in an atmosphere of broken promises, of wrecked estates, of neglected trusts, of unperformed duties, of crimes and of quarrels*; these are instantly identifiable as 'Wilsonian' concerns, microcosms of the much larger concerns that lay behind the Fourteen Points.[10]

It took more romantic turns as well. While at Atlanta, Wilson met and fell in love with Ellen Axson, the daughter of a Georgia clergyman. Ellen was intelligent and lively and seems to have countered Wilson's prejudice against women as intellectual equals (though this surfaced again when he taught at Bryn Mawr, a college for women). The couple were engaged in September 1883, just as Wilson abandoned his law practice and enrolled as a graduate student at Johns Hopkins University in Baltimore. With one profession set aside, marriage would have to wait until Wilson finished his doctorate.

Johns Hopkins was modelled on the great European universities, with an emphasis on individual development rather than curricular rigour. Wilson enrolled as a history student, but his work veered to the political, with the apparent approval of his supervisor, Professor Herbert Baxter Adams. Inspired by a fresh reading of Bagehot, he embarked on a book that would, he unconvincingly claimed, emphasise the *exegetical* rather than the *evangelical*.[11] Both those words would be familiar to a Presbyterian clergyman's son, but whereas his strongly advocated 'Cabinet Government' essay adopted the latter approach, what became *Congressional Government* was essentially descriptive. Essentially, but not entirely, because implicit in Wilson's exegesis was a comparison with the British system and an insistence that without a strictly accountable central focus of government – like the British cabinet – carrying on its work in full visibility and with a *dignifying* [very much a Bagehot word!] *and elevating sense of being trusted* there was no potential for decisive political action. For Wilson, perhaps even more than for Bagehot and with a stronger moral connotation, the 'dignified' went hand-in-hand with the 'efficient'.[12] In later years Wilson invested less in the role of cabinet than in the office of the presidency itself as the source of political authority; this was the thrust of a later, indeed his last

THE AMERICAN PARTY SYSTEM

In addition to warning Americans against foreign entanglements, George Washington's 'Farewell Address' of 1796 counselled a clear-minded avoidance of the purely regional interests and consequent 'jealousies and heart-burnings' that would come from political parties. The sentiment was echoed by James Madison in the tenth paper of *The Federalist* in 1787 when he defended the American Constitution's system of checks and balances as the best protection against the worst excesses of party spirit.

However, party divisions rapidly developed, partly as the legacy of the British polarisation of Whig and Tory philosophies, but largely due to the vast geographical scale of America and conflict of regional interests: Northern and Southern, and somewhat later, Atlantic and Western. The very scale of the United States also meant that when an essentially party system did develop (largely as the result of direct election to the presidency), each grouping was required to offer the broadest possible manifesto to the electorate and with less ideological consistency over time than was usual with European political parties.

The Democratic Party emerged out of the confusingly named Democratic-Republican wing of American politics, organised behind Madison and Thomas Jefferson, who supported states' rights in opposition to the centralising policies of the Federalists. In the 'Revolution of 1800', Vice-President Jefferson defeated President John Adams; the Federalist Party declined rapidly and disbanded after the war of 1812. The Democratic-Republican interest then split into Jeffersonian Democrats, with a largely agrarian philosophy, and Whigs, who in turn were riven by the slavery question.

The Republican Party emerged out of a growing North-South divide

important book *Constitutional Government in the United States*, published in 1908 when he was president of Princeton and already identified as a candidate for the Presidency itself. It is also implicit in lectures like 'Leaders of Men', given at Wesleyan shortly before he left and in which he makes a distinction between the visionary/literary and more ruthlessly pragmatic qualities required in some balance for effective leadership. One should not read too much into his apparent unwillingness to call regular cabinet meetings while

on the slavery question, with disaffected Northern – or 'War' – Democrats gravitating to Abraham Lincoln's Republican National Union Party. Southern Democrats rallied in opposition to the post-bellum Reconstruction. The Democratic party did not return a president until 1884, when Grover Cleveland was elected for the first of two non-consecutive terms on a ticket which was pro-business, and committed to a gold standard, low taxes and the elimination of corruption. The so-called 'Bourbon Democrats' were displaced by the neo-Jeffersonian agrarian and pro-silver philosophy of William Jennings Bryan who stood twice for the presidency.

After the split of the Republican Party in 1912, and under the liberal-progressive philosophy of Woodrow Wilson, the Democratic Party moved to the left of the Republicans, a position it has occupied to this day, permanently weakening any third-party interest (Populist or Socialist) which might compete for the same constituency.

Madison's confidence in the system of checks and balances was based on the notion that states' rights would protect individual states both from each other and from central government and that the system of election – particularly the electoral college and the careful diversification of tenure through the different branches of government – would prevent sudden disruptive changes in political feeling which might overtake the country as a whole. Congressmen serve for two years, Senators for six (with only one-third of the Senate coming up for election at a time), and the President for four. Wilson's thinking, in *Congressional Government* and elsewhere, and his experience with Republican majorities in Congress in 1918 reflect the complexity of this situation and his ambivalence towards it.

president; during his first administration, Wilson practised collective responsibility, delegating confidently; the first two years of his second term were passed under extraordinary circumstances; at the end of his political life, he was physically and emotionally frail, and only felt comfortable with intimates. Even so, there was a sharp evolution in Wilson's thinking between his early theoretical writing and his later, more practical approach. In the shift, he helped reform the modern presidency.

It might be tempting to say that in his first administration Wilson practised what he had preached in *Congressional Government* because though his style falls short of the evangelical, it is certainly not a work of disinterested exegesis, nor one that draws on empirical research. The standard criticisms of Wilson's most important book – and these must stretch in some measure to his entire political career – are that it is essentially a work of persuasion, a rhetorical assertion of an ideal political system rather than an analysis of a government in action, and that it was written in the library rather than in the public galleries of Congress. The latter criticism is objectively justified, since Wilson made no attempt to study American governance at first hand. (His wartime Secretary of State Robert Lansing complained that Wilson was not interested in facts, only in big ideas and abstract principles, and the charge is equally well founded.) On the other hand, Wilson believed that there was a uniquely fruitful relationship in politics between iconic constitutional texts – the United States was a country, after all, founded on text – that were susceptible to interpretation if not change, and the factitious reality of actual lives lived in the mass. Wilson understood that the first was, in some sense, an expression and distillation of the second, responsive to it, but only through a highly specialised layer of language. For Wilson, the role of the politician was to give shape to the inchoate needs, ambitions and fears of the populace, to cast them in a form that addressed the common weal in a way not only practical but also persuasive enough to bring the people into line behind it. This was Wilson's method throughout his career: the sick man who spoke at Pueblo in 1919 was no more a pragmatist and no less an idealist than the newly elected president in 1912 or the reforming Princeton academic administrator a decade earlier. He rejected populism absolutely as mere bending with the wind. Wilson had imbibed enough evolutionary theory at Johns Hopkins – this, perhaps, the intellectual adventure that distanced him most from his upbringing: Darwin remained a hate name in the South – to believe that the standard Whig model of history as a self-regulating engine with a single sense of direction was less convincing than one based on capricious, and sometimes retrograde, changes in the development of a living system. Though his emphasis on education and journalism as the first and primary stage in social and political change mark him down as a product of the age, Wilsonism marks the end of the Progressive era in American history partly because Wilson himself adopted a more holistic, though neither tragic nor quietistic, acceptance of social evolution as multi-faceted, complex and sometimes perverse. Critically, the more he accepted this, the more he emphasised the need for strong central authority and the more he extolled leadership the more he found himself identified – and perhaps identified himself – as a potential future leader. If the law did not prove to be the natural route to a political role, teaching and writing did.

Unhampered by trips to Washington, Wilson finished his book by the autumn of 1884 and by the following January it was published and receiving enthusiastic – and in some cases, hyperbolic – reviews. These helped establish his reputation nationally, but they also had another outcome. In 1886, the graduate board at Johns Hopkins accepted *Congressional Government* in lieu of a thesis, and the positive opinion of its reviewers in place of tough *viva* questions, and awarded him his Ph.D. By this time, though, Wilson was no longer at John Hopkins, though he returned frequently to lecture over the next decade. He wished to marry and a married man needed a career. The wedding was in June 1885, after which Wilson took up a teaching post at Bryn Mawr College in Massachusetts. Arguably, Bryn Mawr was no more of a finishing school for New England ladies than Johns Hopkins was for Southern gentlemen; the school's guiding feminism gave the curriculum more rigour than Wilson, however courtly and respectful, was willing to concede. Though it may simply be that Wilson, always dependent on sympathy, support and a strong measure of fellow-feeling with his colleagues, was unable to get along with Dean Carey Thomas, who ran the Bryn Mawr faculty, he did express an urge to work in a more rugged intellectual and social environment. There was also perhaps some irony in teaching the theory of government to young women who were not yet enfranchised; not until the end of Wilson's presidency, with the 19th Amendment in 1920, did women get the vote. In 1888 he accepted a post at Wesleyan University in Connecticut, where at least there was baseball instead of lacrosse.

The Wilsons had two daughters by this time: Margaret and Jessie were born in 1886 and 1887, a third girl, Eleanor, in 1889. Home life seems to have been happy, a view confirmed by Ellen's brother Stockton Axson, also an academic, who wrote a (slightly self-serving) memoir of *'Brother Woodrow'* that was eventually published in 1993. Along with his father, who lived long enough to see Wilson installed at Princeton in 1902, this was the first circle of intimacy; students and trusted colleagues were the next; wider recognition was growing, though, through his books – *The State* was published in 1889, a comparative treatment of modern and classical models that became a valued textbook – and articles – George Harvey of *Harper's* magazine became a valuable supporter and sponsor – and also through guest appearances at Johns Hopkins, where Wilson gave lectures on administration. His health seems to have been good at this period, or at least giving no cause for comment or alarm.

In 1890, the stage suddenly grew broader and higher: Woodrow Wilson (this was when the Thomas disappeared for good) returned to Princeton – still the College of New Jersey – as Professor of Jurisprudence and Political Economy. His productivity, in and out of the classroom, certainly suggests vigour. Wilson came back to his old school with a growing reputation and his classes were enthusiastically subscribed, creating over a dozen years a substantial constituency of talented young men who remembered him with admiration and affection, an intellectual coach who shaped many influential public careers. He wrote steadily as well, publishing the excellent *Division and Reunion, 1829–1889* in 1893 and a study of George Washington three years later. The latter was intended as a popular biography of the first president – and fellow-Virginian – but it also develops some of the ideas on leadership that were occupying Wilson through this period. As a child of the Civil War and Reconstruction period, and a Southern child at that, Wilson had observed with dismay the deterioration of the post-bellum presidency. Candidates were increasingly pliable mouthpieces for party interests rather than the disinterested, Cincinnatus-like figures of the early republic. In addition, the political impeachment of Andrew Johnson and the corruption of the Grant administration had weakened both the actual authority and public perception of the office.

As Wilson put the final touches to his Washington book, the College was completing its translation into Princeton University; its academic and scholarly transformation lagged somewhat behind and would ultimately depend on the rising star of the faculty. In the summer of 1896, though, Wilson's health was giving cause for concern. In May, he suffered either a minor stroke or transient ischaemic attack (TIA) which restricted the mobility of his right hand. A decade later, to the month, he suffered a similar attack, which left him temporarily blind in one eye. On both occasions, a family holiday in the Lake District helped recover his health, while visits to both Oxford and Cambridge impressed him deeply; on both occasions he returned to work with new ideas and with vigour almost alarmingly redoubled. In the autumn of 1896, Wilson delivered the sesquicentennial address at the university: 'Princeton in the Nation's Service' nailed his colours firmly to the mast; the title later became the university motto.

A man without independent fortune must ... content himself with becoming an outside force in politics... .
WOODROW WILSON LETTER TO ELLEN AXSON, 30 OCTOBER 1883.[13]

Six years later, he was giving that 'prime ministerial' inaugural address he wrote of to Ellen – it bore the near-identical name 'Princeton for the Nation's Service' – as incoming university president. Wilson was the first lay figure to hold the post. His predecessor, the Rev Dr Francis Patton, was squeezed out by the trustees due to his resistance to reform. Wilson came in with just such a programme, aiming to develop undergraduate education on the basis of a broad and coherent foundation course, and to turn an inward-looking Presbyterian institution, where the faculty were mostly alumni and the student body – apart from those engaged on vocational courses in the Theological Seminary – relatively uninterested in learning, into a seat of learning whose main imperative was to produce a cohort of future leaders.

Wilson proselytised among former Princeton men and

fundraised vigorously. His aim was to more than double the university endowment in order to fund the 50 new tutors he required for a new 'preceptorial' system that would replace the existing, at-a-distance method of 'lectures and quizzes'. Typically, he set about these changes before the money was forthcoming, though he could count on a rich college friend to underwrite any shortfall. In January 1903, Wilson had a personal setback, when his father, who had been living with the family, passed away. There were more clouds on the professional horizon. After introducing the preceptors, Wilson wanted to reform the eating clubs that were at the heart of Princeton student life and convert them into Oxbridge-like collegiate 'quads' which would fall under university control. This was, of course, the sticking point and Wilson met with stiff resistance, some of it undoubtedly personal in nature; after the Rev Dr Patton, he must have seemed decidedly un-Princetonian in manner and approach. As with his later attempts to defend the League, Wilson's efforts redoubled the more improbable success seemed and the strain of endless politicking and speaking took a toll on his health; the 1906 stroke came at the height of the controversy.

Wilson nearly resigned, but as with a later controversy over the location of a new Graduate School – on-campus or at some distance – and the issues of finance and control that went with it, he was constitutionally unable to give up on a position or to concede either defeat or the possibility that he might be in the wrong. Wilson's Princeton career marks an important foreshadowing of his national and international political career, not so much because there are serious parallels between the organisation of a campus and the running of a country, between a squabble over a grad school and a European war with global implications, or between an endowment

from American history, it looks as if his entire career and reputation were based on a single reckless moment in the Spanish-American War, a much-publicised but militarily not very significant charge up San Juan Hill in Cuba, with his legendary Rough Riders, a relatively trivial engagement that nonetheless won TR a posthumous Medal of Honour – something he passionately coveted – in 2001, more than 80 years after he died. In his final years, he was eager to prove that his charge hadn't been a fluke. He was furious when, in 1917, Wilson denied him his wish to lead a division in France; nothing sharpened the animosity between Wilson and Roosevelt as much as that, as doubtless it was intended to do, for Roosevelt was a master of what is now called political spin.

If he was an action hero and outdoorsman, friend of the Scottish-born environmentalist John Muir, it was as the result of dogged and painful exercise to build up a weak and shrivelled childhood frame. Cecil Spring-Rice had considered his mind childlike, and some of his actions – even to the suggestion that he might fight on the Western Front – do sound adolescent. However, Roosevelt was possessed of a vigorous and lively intellect and was also author of a number of books, though they tended more to Western history than to constitutional theory. His Christianity was as orthodox as Wilson's, albeit more obviously muscular, and it may well be that the rich New Yorker saw politics as the working-out of the Gospels more than did the son of the manse. By whatever measure, Roosevelt was a president with genuine charisma and a galvanising personal style. He ended the long post-Lincoln line of suspect nonentities and party placemen and proved to be, under the carefully manufactured exterior, as pragmatic and able a politician as Wilson. He restored something to the office, though perhaps not in quite the manner

Wilson imagined. He also had something in the first decade of the century that Wilson did not: Roosevelt had learned his politics in the tough and no-nonsense world of New York Republicanism, where scorn for Democratic corruption and malpractice was worn like a tie-pin; in contrast, Wilson was running a gentlemen's college, and was more immediately known for having lost a politely bitter squabble over the location and funding of a graduate school than he was for *Constitutional Government in the United States,* which appeared towards the end of his tenure at Princeton in 1908.

That was an election year. In keeping with tradition (later enshrined in the constitution after Franklin D Roosevelt, a nephew by marriage and fifth cousin, shortly to become an aide in the Wilson administration, overturned it), TR had decided not to stand for a further term, effectively his third, though it would only have been his second as an elected president. He had been returned – and vindicated – four years before, returning to the White House with a handsome majority and defeating in the process William Jennings Bryan, one of American politics' most persistent second-place man. Bryan, who became Wilson's Secretary of State but then split with him over the war issue, had been a Democratic inspiration in 1896, but by 1908 had become its sheet-anchor, running short of energy and credibility, memories of his famous 'Cross of Gold' speech a long way distant, holding back the process of party reform and modernisation, associated with an unrealistic Southern rearguard.

By contrast, Wilson had turned himself into a *de facto* Northerner, in political method if not in manner or style. His enthusiastic embrace of evolutionary theory as a model of political change was the strongest sign of both his modernity and his willingness to set aside the usual Southern Democratic tropes in favour of a new and electable configuration for the party. Wilson's grooming for political office was undertaken largely by conservative Northern Democrats, even if he didn't entirely share their views; originally an admirer of Grover Cleveland, he moved somewhat, if inconsistently, leftward during his time at Princeton. In 1908, he was quite clearly still unqualified for high office, but after securing from him an indication that he would consider standing – it was *Harper's* editor George Harvey, an admirer and sponsor, who seems to have asked the key question – the party set about grooming him for 1912.

Wilson walked away from Princeton having lost a battle with Dean West over the location and funding of the Graduate School but having gained considerable standing from having fought his corner and making what to most bluecollar Americans must have seemed an obscure academic squabble into a resigning issue. He walked out of academia in order to fulfil his earliest conviction – one in which Ellen stoutly supported him – that political office was his *métier.* One of the reasons Wilson's politics are difficult to unravel, either viewed over time or else at any given moment as a bundle of principles and promises, is that the nature, the holding and the exercise of political office was always more important to him than specific policies. Wilson talked often of expediency, but in both positive and negative contexts. He talked somewhat of *the people* in the semi-mystical tone of American Populism (though he welcomed the rise of a new and carefully qualified *sober public opinion* [my emphasis]), and he deplored the elitism of the Northern political establishment, but he dismissed Bryan's address to the people as mere expediency and he at times advocated a strongly centralist – or Federalist – approach to politics.[1] In *Congressional Government* Wilson claimed that even the Founding Fathers would have to concede that *the only fruit of dividing power had been to make it irresponsible* and that the *'literary theory'* of checks and balances in the constitution was not much more than that.

To be fair to Wilson, at the time he was emerging onto a national political stage, he still had some Southern dust on his shoes, and the rarefied atmosphere of Princeton, even at the height of the funding squabble, was not sufficiently dynamic to blow it off. His potential weakness was the same as the weakness, actual and perceived, of *Congressional Government*, that it was theoretically sophisticated, rhetorically subtle, but innocent of the day-to-day workings of government. In addition, Wilson was coming into politics at a moment when the great industrial and fiscal boom that had been the solid fuel of Progressivism was giving way to jitters and when there was a persistent unease about the political system itself; machines had taken over in both places and where formerly Wilson would have identified socialists and saboteurs (machine-wreckers) as the greatest threat to the democracy, now he was increasingly inclined to see the big trusts and plutocrats as the enemy within. To this extent, he was in tune with the times.

His appeal to the Democratic Party was largely that he *was* an outsider, someone untainted by contact with the hated 'machines', but also someone who seemed both wedded to resounding principle but sufficiently pliable to serve the needs of the party. When, at Harvey's behest and over the reservations of party figures who considered him professorial and perhaps too haughty, Wilson was approached as a potential candidate for the New Jersey governorship he enthusiastically embraced a broad platform of progressive reforms proposed by the local party and won a resounding victory in November

1910, in line with strong Democratic gains in both houses of Congress. If Wilson's reformist promises perturbed his conservative backers, and particularly his pledge to reform the very system of placements and patronage they had erected, it bothered them less than it might, given the understanding, which Wilson had made clear and public, that the priority was the presidential nomination in 1912. The climax of his gubernatorial campaign was an unscripted extra speech to an enthusiastic crowd where he declared: *America is not distinguished so much by its wealth and material power as by the fact that it was born with an idea, a purpose to serve mankind.* This was not the rhetoric associated with a state election; this was a man already running for the White House in his head.

America is not distinguished so much by its wealth and material power as by the fact that it was born with an idea, a purpose to serve mankind.
WOODROW WILSON

More acutely, those same Democratic regulars had also received assurances from Wilson that he would not attempt to replace the existing Democratic machinery. This was a clever hedge, for it didn't quite distance him from a pledge to party activists that he would clean out the Augean stables of political corruption. The term was a notably mobile one: what seemed like corruption to one set of interests was simply the normal way of doing business to another. Wilson, perhaps aware that if the auguries continued to be auspicious he would be moving on to bigger things in less than two years – his presidential campaign office opened in July 1911 – was happy to promise that he would not replace the existing machine with one of his own.

He was equally happy, once in office, to resist the 'normal' workings of the Democracy in New Jersey. One of his first as a eloquent proponent that marked his term. With Smith robbed of his power base and party chairman James Nugent set aside, it was easier for Wilson to go after the corrupt party machines; the fury of the old guard was palpable, and if they could not claim the moral high ground, they were somewhat justified in thinking that Wilson had welched on a promise.

In a foretaste of 1919, but in cooler weather and happier circumstances, Wilson went on a speaking tour of the Midwest in the spring of 1911, advocating a programme of anti-corporation measures and legislative amendment to state constitutions in order to prevent vested interests exerting covert control. It was a platform that squared comfortably with Bryan's now shop-worn message and was in large part constructed in order to win over 'the Great Commoner' and his still-loyal but electorally drifting constituency. Reactions to Wilson were still tumultuous in 1919, but his audiences came on an ebbing tide. In 1912, it was overwhelmingly with him.

His presidential campaign was partly funded by Cleveland H Dodge, who had underwritten Wilson's reforms at Princeton, and was run from New York by William Gibbs McAdoo, a brilliant businessman who subsequently became Wilson's Treasury secretary, and by William F McCombs, a young lawyer and former student who, like Tumulty admired Wilson immoderately and offered his boss unqualified support, ironically given what happened after the election. Something similar came from House, who bore the honorary title of Colonel, and became the man in whom Wilson confided his strongest – sometimes contradictory – feelings, his ambitions and his anxieties. Together, though McAdoo and McCombs later feuded, they represented a human palisade, not so much yes-men, as men of affairs who brokered a relationship between Wilson and both party and people.

Unfortunately, the people were about to deal Wilson a blow. Having ostensibly backed his desire to reform political practice and move ahead on a broad progressive platform, the New Jersey electorate returned a Republican majority to both houses in the state legislature. This time, Wilson's reputation was damaged rather than enhanced by his proudly principled stand. Fortunately, help was at hand from an unexpected source. As mentioned above, the 1912 conventions were the first in which party primaries had a determining role; both winning candidates would campaign for their extension to the presidential elections as well. On the Republican side, Roosevelt secured a relatively easy win, but after a number of delegates were challenged, the nomination was handed to incumbent president William H Taft, who represented the conservative wing. In a fury that clinched the 'Bull Moose' label he took to the polls the following autumn, Roosevelt stormed out of the Republican party on the evening of 22 June 1912; the Republican vote was now split between Taft and the new Progressive Party.

Wilson's own travails were not over, however. The Democratic Party, riven more by regional than by strictly ideological interests, had put up 13 nominees, of whom two, apart from Wilson, stood as strong contenders: both Southerners and both with considerable political experience. Champ Clark of Missouri was the House Speaker, while Oscar Underwood of Alabama spoke for the Cleveland-inspired conservative wing Wilson had left behind in his steady evolution toward a more liberal mission for the Democracy. Wilson would have been a near-automatic choice against a united Republican Party, but after the defection of the Bull Moose loyalists, sectional interests began to play a part again: the conclusion was that a Democratic victor was almost a foregone conclusion, but the internecine struggle that followed was potentially as damaging to the Democrats as Roosevelt's outright secession had been to the other side.

Wilson lost ground in the primaries, and went into the party convention seriously weakened and facing a potentially hostile chairman, a Northern conservative. Clark had a majority of delegate votes, but not enough to claim to the two-thirds he required for a win. Wilson seemed ready to concede, a decision supported by his backers, but he decided not to give his supporters a free vote. Underwood stayed in the race, and the contest moved behind the scenes as deals were struck and concessions offered. Denied his last chance to be king, Bryan tried to play kingmaker and offered carefully hedged and qualified support for Wilson; but it took further horse-trading and nearly 50 convention ballots to push the former professor over the finishing line.

Against Theodore Roosevelt, it was imperative that the Democrats put up a candidate who appealed to the mass of the people. Wilson was that man; and yet it was clear that Wilson's appeal was of a radically different order, still inchoate and rhetorical, unfashioned by deed, abstract and philosophical rather than forceful and willed. His words had presence, but compared to the manufactured image of 'TR', the bear-hunting (but bear-sparing) Rough Rider and Bull Moose, he did not. Roosevelt even contrived to survive an assassination attempt in Milwaukee during the campaign, saved by a spectacles case and the thick speech in his coat pocket; he went ahead with his speech, blood oozing through his shirt. Wilson's only possible response was to suspend electioneering until TR recovered. Taft, who lost his running mate Vice-President James S Sherman a week before the polls, campaigned resignedly and the

PROGRESSIVISM

'Progressivism' refers to a congeries of social, political and educational philosophies that emerged in the period of rapid industrial growth towards the end of the 19th century – and very largely as a response to it – but which has a particular connotation in an American context.

The 'Progressive Era' in the United States takes in the administrations of Theodore Roosevelt, William H Taft and Woodrow Wilson. Its chief concern was social justice and resistance to vested interest but the period also saw an attempt to broaden and democratize the electoral process and to render it more accountable. Among the more significant measures instituted were direct election of senators by the voting populace rather than by state legislatures (the 17th Amendment to the Constitution, introduced in 1911, met with strong resistance from North-Eastern Republicans and was only ratified by all states in April 1913, under Wilson's administration), the introduction of direct primaries and referenda, as well as 'initiative' (the introduction of legislation by the state populace) and the principle of 'recall' by which an elected official could be removed from office.

The proliferation of state and government business in the post Civil War period had not been matched by efficiencies in administration, but had tended to institutionalise corruption and malpractice. These were major concerns of the 'Progressive Era'. Progressivism also recognised that the rapid growth of industrial society had led to specific social problems (homelessness, urban poverty, physical displacement) and a need to protect land, and particularly wilderness, from runaway development. In addition to settlement projects and more enlightened labour laws, a conservation movement emerged during the Roosevelt administration.

Some historians have suggested that 'progressive' is an almost empty term, but inconsistent as it sometimes was in application, it expresses a new confidence in American society.

veteran Socialist candidate Eugene V Debs had his own distinct constituency (though in the event he increased his vote impressively). It was widely understood that this was to be a two-horse race, and with one reformer set against another, Roosevelt's 'New Nationalism' against Wilson's 'New Freedom'; given how interchangeable some of the manifesto elements were, fine differences of policy would count for a great deal.

While Wilson's calls for strong leadership worked somewhat against the grain of a traditional Democratic suspicion of big government, his growing suspicion of big business offered more promising electoral ground. Business had been the engine of the Progressive era, but business had also acquired a thoroughly undemocratic level of political influence and the nominated targets of Wilson's campaign – in contrast to Roosevelt's embrace of big business and faith in federal regulation – were corporations, trusts and monopolies, sharpening a dialectic that would dominate American politics into the Depression era. It was constructed on a subtly balanced question: how to regulate the very sector that made the country prosperous and strong and keep America from the fate of the Sorcerer's Apprentice.

When Wilson named his first cabinet, the most startling omission was the name of Louis D Brandeis, the brilliant anti-corporation lawyer who had helped to shape Wilson's thinking and policy on regulation. The decision, made at House's insistent recommendation, was pure expediency; though a liberal hero, and admired by Bryan, Brandeis was also a controversial and much-disliked figure. Wilson adopted many of his ideas and built them into a campaign that delivered some of the finest – and most impressively unified – political oratory of the 20th century. Freedom, at the level of the individual, was its keyword. Again and again, he promoted the wishes and ambitions of the ordinary voter and dedicated himself to the promulgation of *laws that will give the little man a start, that will give him a chance to show these fellows that he has brains enough to compete with them and can presently make his local market a national market and his*

THOMAS R MARSHALL (1854–1925)

'What this country really needs is a good five-cent cigar.' Vice-President Thomas R Marshall's witticism is almost his only contribution to posterity. Wilson largely excluded Marshall from the business of government and there seems to have been little warmth between the two men. However, Marshall was the first vice-president to be re-elected for a second term since Daniel D Tompkins, who served under James Monroe from 1817 to 1825, and the first to win all the same states as the president during the election, a situation which is now considered the norm.

Two years older than Wilson, Marshall was an Indiana lawyer and subsequently the state governor (1909–13), during which time he attempted to introduce progressive legislation. He originally resisted nomination for the vice-presidency, thinking (correctly) that the job would afford few challenges. He seems to have regarded Wilson as cold and buttoned-up, once presenting him with the gift of a book inscribed 'From your only Vice', and Wilson in turn rarely invited him to cabinet meetings and abandoned the practice of using the Vice-President as a go-between to the Senate. Marshall sometimes asked White House visitors to throw nuts to him, implying that he was kept largely as a pet.

After Wilson's paralytic stroke, there was uncertainty as to correct procedure when a president became incapacitated, and in practice Edith Wilson and the inner circle largely excluded Marshall. He was, however, an effective speaker and during the war addressed war bond rallies in the Midwest with impressive results. His pawky manner and no-nonsense practicality made him an ideal foil for Wilson, and his remark about the cigar (if he ever actually said it) guaranteed him a place in the record.

national market a world market. No was left in doubt who 'these fellows' were, but what is interesting about Wilson's rhetoric is the assumed continuum between individual enterprise and global impact.

In asserting this, Wilson drew an implicit contrast between the Progressives' desire to fix America in the moment and to draw blinds and shutters over the windows on the 'city on a hill' that has been invoked by nearly every president and presidential hopeful in the republic's history, instead of letting them shine forth as an example and as a promise to the world. He spoke from scripts, but also extemporaneously when ovations grew so protracted that he was obliged either to deviate from his text or to speak again. He could not match Roosevelt's bravura, but relied instead on a subtle modulation from calm explication to high passion, the exegetical giving way once again to the evangelical. If his delivery was still to a degree professorial, his campaign speeches often have the pace and cadence of a sermon.

The 1912 election was the first in American history in which an incumbent president was beaten into third place. In the event, Taft did not do as badly as might have been expected. His three and a half million popular votes fell just short of Roosevelt's at just over four million. Debs nearly doubled his vote, to nearly 6 per cent. Wilson won a plurality, with just over six and a quarter million votes. In the electoral college, however, he received 435 votes, to Roosevelt's 88 and Taft's eight. The 'Princeton schoolmaster' was elected 28th President of the United States.

ooooo

Wilson was a minority president – Bryan had received a larger percentage four years earlier – but a proportion of those who voted for Roosevelt must have cast their ballot for the Democrats in the Congressional elections; having won the House of Representatives in 1910, Wilson's party now controlled the Senate as well, a situation he regarded as essential for stable, consistent government. His mandate was further strengthened by the recognition that ten million Americans had voted for a reformist candidate. In the final balance, Wilson's individualism had won out over Roosevelt's regulatory paternalism (and Debs's utopianism).

According to the new president installed in office the following March, credit for his victory went not to party, or to people, or even to a close-knit campaign team. It is the unfortunate duty of political subordinates to douse euphoria with practicality and to remind the victor that politics is a patronage business and that favours have to be repaid. As head of the Democratic national committee, whose post-war memoir was entitled *Making Woodrow Wilson President,* McCombs had a list of those who would claim a place at the White House table. It must have been discomfiting to find that he was not one of them. According to McCombs, who may have been trying to convey an attitude rather than Wilson's actual words, the President brushed him aside with the words *God ordained that I should be the next president of the United States .... I owe you nothing.*

God ordained that I should be the next president of the United States ...
WOODROW WILSON

Even with providence at his back, and with a determination to run government from the White House, Wilson was shrewd enough to know that he needed to delegate somewhat and was required to recognise some of those who had helped put him in office. Brandeis and House were not given official positions, the former because it would have been politically inflammatory, the latter because he seems to have preferred it that way; both remained as personal advisers, though later, in January 1916, Wilson outraged conservatives by appointing Brandeis to the Supreme Court, the first Jew ever to sit there. As a Catholic, Tumulty was equally suspect in the South, but he remained a behind-the-scenes factotum. William B Wilson (no relation) was made Secretary of Labour and Albert S Burleson Postmaster-General. McAdoo was given the Treasury, and Josephus Daniels from North Carolina, who had handled Democratic publicity during the campaign, was made Secretary of the Navy, an astonishing appointment given that a less warlike personality could scarcely have been found. The oddity of the choice suggests how little importance Wilson place on international affairs at this point. That impression is confirmed by his agreement (under some pressure) to reward Bryan for his distinguished service with the post of Secretary of State. This created an interesting situation, because Bryan – like Burleson, who had hundreds of jobs at his disposal with which to reward the party faithful – was in favour of patronage and gave potentially important, and particularly so after 1914, foreign service jobs to unqualified individuals. This compromised a slow improvement in that sector and had an immediate impact on American attitudes and response when war broke out, as will be seen.

American foreign policy in 1912 was still dominated by two cherished principles set down in what is known as Washington's Farewell Address (actually a published statement distributed to newspapers and broadsheets) and in the Monroe Doctrine. As he left office, the first president had warned America of the dangers of overseas entanglement, and urged the country to look inward. Bryan, a Nebraskan, was unusual for the time in taking a lively, if slightly eccentric interest in foreign affairs.

Roosevelt had made his reputation fighting (albeit briefly, and with more dash than strategic vision) in the Spanish-American War of 1898, America's first armed conflict for half a century. This was, though, in keeping with the Monroe Doctrine's assertion that the Americas as a whole were the

United States' sphere of influence; New Left historians tended to interpret that as a rationalisation for American economic and political dominance; Woodrow Wilson later reinterpreted the Doctrine as a rational *modus vivendi* for neighbouring nations and recommended its spirit to the warring powers in Europe. Under McKinley, though, the principle was geographically extended to include the annexation of Hawaii, Puerto Rico, Guam and the Philippines (places which have resonated strongly in American political, military and social history ever since) and the establishment of a protectorate in Cuba (ditto); while the so-called Open Door policy on China's territorial and political integrity and an operatically famous mission to Japan asserted American interest (half-highmindedness, half-expediency) in the Far East. As president, Roosevelt had helped broker a peace treaty between Japan and Russia after the war of 1904–5, and received the Nobel Peace Prize for his efforts; he also, perhaps more unusually, sent delegates to the Algeciras Conference in 1906. For the most part, though, America's view of the world, and particularly of Europe was determined by George Washington's insistence on 'no entangling alliances'. The New World viewed the Old through Henry James's spectacles: Europe was complex, cunning, riven with plots and double-dealing, culturally rich but morally and politically decadent; America was bright, forward-looking, innocent, resistant to cabals, still fresh with promise. The average American knew little of the outside world and cared less. There was an unspoken understanding that a foreign policy was strictly unnecessary, or was simply a rhetorical flourish, useful for inaugurals and Independence Day speeches when, in Hugh Brogan's striking phrase 'it was thought desirable to let the eagle scream a little'.[2]

Wilson was both typical and in one important respect untypical in his attitude to Europe at the time of taking office. His cabinet appointments suggest strongly that not only did he consider it undesirable that America should be drawn into 'entangling' commitments to any of the European powers, but also unlikely. Nevertheless, he was a strong Anglophile with an instinctive sympathy for British ways and for British ways of thinking. Whenever he faced defeat, Ellen consoled him with the thought that at least they could visit his beloved Lake District again. Ellen's death, from Bright's disease, came just two days after the war in Europe broke out; Wilson was denied her consoling presence and also denied the consolation – which he may not have wished in any case – of following a wholly American path in his administration. His only active military deployment in 1914 was the occupation of Vera Cruz in Mexico, where a volatile revolution had for three years threatened the stability and equanimity of the South-Western states. General John Pershing (1860–1938), who later would lead the American forces in France, led a punitive raid in 1916 after Pancho Villa launched an attack on Columbus, New Mexico.

These were actions readily understood and largely supported by the American population. Involvement in the European war was equally largely unthinkable. However, there is evidence that Wilson considered it both inevitable and desirable, and in a foretaste of his government's vigorous propagandising against 'Communists' and 'hyphenates' at the end of the war he encouraged anti-German propaganda and atrocity stories, conscious that his ancestral loyalties were not those of many million Americans, whose roots and sympathies lay with the Central Powers. It is commonly thought that the German submarine campaign, directed against 'neutral' shipping, was the single main cause of America's entering the war. This, and notably the sinking of the *Lusitania*, which is discussed in the next chapter, did have an impact, both economic and human. However, very few Americans travelled abroad at the time – it is estimated that fewer than 10 per cent of Americans have passports in the present decade; the figure may have been slightly higher in the 1910s given less stringent security regulations and closer familial ties to the European homelands – and the risks were both known and, until the *Lusitania*, relatively small. One of the profoundest sticking points at the Peace Conference was the freedom of the seas. For most of the period since Trafalgar and the end of the French wars, it was understood that the Royal Navy controlled the oceans, a shield to Empire and an enforcer of economic hegemony. America's entry into the First World War started the erosion of that authority. Wilson's natural Anglophilia – and instinctive desire to join the conflict in the Allied interest – was stalled somewhat by a growing suspicion of Britain's claim to the oceans, in part by irritation that the Royal Navy could not deal with the submarine and mine menace, in large part by a strong Austro-German lobby at home, and to an almost incalculable degree by the fact that the war made America a banker to the world, and most critically to the cash-poor United Kingdom. This was controversial enough to question the nature of American 'neutrality' right from the beginning.

Wilson's position on the war, his involvement in the Peace Conference and in the formation of the League of Nations have largely eclipsed his earlier domestic achievement, and if the former can be characterised as compromise and defeat, the latter produced some significant advances that reshaped aspects of American life ever after. As ever, though, Wilson was as much concerned with the form and function of political life as with the content of specific policies. Thomas Jefferson had abandoned the practice of going to Congress to recommend legislation and report on the state of the nation. Wilson was as attracted as many of his opponents were repelled by the symbolic power of a 'royal' speech to parliament, which in Britain is written by the government of the day and delivered by the monarch. Wilson's own sense of divine right, though, was mitigated by a genuine desire *not* to seem an isolated and remote figure of executive of power and more positively to do as he had always done and address men directly and face to face, rather than have a congressional clerk read out the speech in a clerkish voice. Whether the benches relished the prospect of being preached to can only be imagined, but Wilson had history and precedent working on his side, and his administration, coinciding as it did with accelerating advance in the mass media, changed the relationship between executive and legislature in America for ever.

There was more to Wilson's willingness to address Congress than the symbolic potency of his being there. He announced that his administration would urgently address the question of tariffs, effectively import taxes, which protected big business against overseas competition. Wilson saw the tariff as the lifeblood of the hated trusts and, again, defined a social good in global rather than merely American terms. Presidential nominee Oscar Underwood, who chaired the House Ways and Means committee and had played a significant role in the Democratic convention, already had a draft bill that reduced tariff rates. The measure encountered fierce opposition from a powerful Washington lobby and Wilson further broke with tradition by making the activities of these interests publicly known. He had insisted that the draft bill be toughened to cover certain agricultural products, but what threatened to alienate Republican progressives like Robert La Follette when the bill reached the Senate was Wilson's practice of politics – his use of Democratic caucuses to drive the measure through – even more than the bill's specific content, which also provided for the introduction of graduated income tax. When the extent of lobby spending by beet-sugar interests was revealed, even defecting Democrats came into line. Wilson signed it into law on 3 October.

Already, he was showing a determination to govern his way. Even if an intellectual coalition of progressives had given him a unified government, Wilson was not prepared to trade with the Republicans and, expediency reigning again, used party machinery to win his desired ends. Wilson's ability to claim the authority of providence also allowed him to be a pragmatist. He did initially hold regular cabinet meetings, but – somewhat contradictorily, given his willingness to make public the activities of the lobby – he was furious when details those meeting were leaked to the press and thereafter relied less heavily on them. He also allowed himself sufficient leisure time not to be overtaken by the hypertension which had stalked him since the two cerebral episodes or the digestive problems that required the use of a stomach pump. On the advice of Dr Cary Grayson, Wilson learned to play golf. His instinct, though, was to centralise. Presidential authority, rather than the 'common counsel' of cabinet, was the best guarantee of fidelity to the cause of common Americans. On the issue of party, he remained necessarily – and forgivably, given the exponentially rising body of work associated with 20th-century administration and legislation – ambivalent. He may have hated machine politics, but he still needed the political machine and his loyalism overtook his utopian wish for a progressive meritocracy; this took its most egregious form – though hardly as ugly in tone as Roosevelt's overt racism – in the replacement of African-American (and mostly Republican) appointees and the steady segregation of the rest.

Two days before Christmas 1913, Wilson signed into law the measure that ultimately allowed the US to fund the Allied war effort. The American banking and currency system was in chaos, but ironically once again it was a divided opposition that allowed Wilson to pass the Federal Reserve Act. Against it were ranged bankers, the anti-bank lobby, states'-rights advocates who feared any measure with 'Federal' in the title, Bryan's agrarian-populism with its need for plentiful paper money and deep suspicion of the Gold Standard. The 'Prosperity at Home, Prestige Abroad' slogan of the McKinley government had come unstuck under his successor with the financial panic of 1907. In that year, Wilson was lecturing at Columbia about the need for free and open world markets, while at home the Republican Senator Nelson Aldrich proposed what would have been the first truly national banking system for the US in some three quarters of a century. The next half decade's argument, leaving aside questions of currency issue and control, was how centralised or how devolved the system should be. The final year of Taft's administration had seen investigation of the so-called 'Money Trust'. The weakness of Aldrich's plan (from a progressive point of view) was that it still left control in private hands. The Democratic chairs of the House and Senate banking and currency committees, Carter Glass from Virginia and Robert Latham Owen from Oklahoma respectively, revived this model, which stood against the kind of centralised system advocated by McAdoo. Wilson's deft, hands-on presentation won over the press and in turn the American people; a carefully calculated measure of cosmetic decentralisation (the Federal Reserve was ultimately a New York-Wall Street fief) suggested enough of the least-worst to bring the sceptical Bryan back on board, and pacify all but a few diehard opponents.

The political and public momentum he gained from general acceptance of the Federal Reserve Act allowed him to move on to what Samuel L Gompers, founder of the American Federation of Labor and an unexpected ally in American preparation for war, referred to as the 'Magna Carta' of labour legislation. Wilson's campaign against the trusts sought to bring an end to restrictive practices and to the simmering conflict between business and government. Again, he showed pragmatism, and good political sense, in disfavouring the kind of anti-trust commission Roosevelt had advocated in the 1912 campaign and putting his authority behind a bill introduced by Congressman Henry Clayton of Alabama, Democratic chairman of the House Judiciary Committee, which declared such practices illegal and subject to criminal proceedings. It was a devastatingly shrewd decision: no innocent man – or more realistically, no innocent company director or employer – could complain; no guilty man would dare to. Wilson signed what became known as the Clayton Anti-Trust Act in October 1914. By then, though, the world was a different place and in ways that must have confirmed Wilson's tacit acceptance of the old Puritan principle of 'as above, so below'. Europe was consumed by war; Wilson himself was a bereft widower.

3

Too proud to fight

Given the elaborate mechanisms of modern American politics, the question of re-election comes round disconcertingly quickly. Ellen's death almost persuaded Wilson not to stand again in 1916. His grief may have had a certain admixture of guilt. During a lone winter holiday in Bermuda a few years earlier, Wilson had met a woman called Mary Peck. It is impossible to tell whether they had a sexual affair or merely an inappropriate friendship (he liked to flirt with women), or to know whether Ellen was aware of the situation, but Wilson suggested that it was a solitary moment of madness and regretted it deeply. There were, however, other factors behind his apparent disinclination to run for a second term. He had probably reached the practical limits of his ability to extend the power of the presidency and was chastened by the awareness that his principled commitment to common counsel was balanced in his administration by the inertial pull of party, regional and personal interest in his government. The congressional elections of 1914 (the first in which senators were directly elected in keeping with the 17th Amendment) left the Senate firmly in Democratic hands, but reduced the majority in the House to just 25; with the inevitability of rebellions on certain issues, and even with the support of progressive Republicans, Wilson could no longer count on an automatic majority there. However, so successful were his first 18 months in office that it was difficult to see what he could possibly promise the American people. History was about to deliver an answer.

In his second inaugural address on 5 March 1917, Wilson described his countrymen as *citizens of the world*, arguing that *the greatest things that remain to be done must be done with the whole world for stage and in cooperation with the wide and universal forces of mankind.*[1] This was not unfamiliar rhetoric from Wilson, but the circumstances were by then dramatically changed. America was already perforce involved in the European conflict. The establishment of the Federal Reserve Bank allowed the United States to bankroll the Allies, and particularly Britain, to a degree which already called into question American 'neutrality'. Less than two decades after an American flag had been planted on Philippine soil, the country was drawn inexorably towards armed conflict on something other than her own terms. Any remaining irritation about British naval high-handedness on the high seas was removed by the German announcement in February 1917 of unrestricted submarine warfare. The sinking of the *Lusitania* two years earlier, and of the *Falaba* and the *Arabic* earlier and later in 1915, had already cost 177 American lives at sea.

Just before his inauguration, Wilson had famously commented to a friend that it would be *the irony of fate* if his administration were to be dominated by foreign affairs.[2] His campaigning had been almost entirely on domestic issues, but having pushed through much of that promised legislation with a Democratic Congress united at his back, Wilson's comment came home to roost. Typically, though, a man who regarded himself as the agent of providence – or fate – did not regard himself as being in the grip of remote and uncontrollable forces. Wilson understood that in matters of foreign policy, the American president acted largely on his own recognisance and with a higher degree of direct authority than he did in domestic affairs. His early efforts in this direction betray a mixture of high-mindedness and naïveté – or at best innocence – but they served as a kind of proving-ground and in the process pushed him toward first indirect, then absolutely direct conflict with Germany.

In 1911, the Mexican dictator Porfirio Diaz had been overthrown. The new leader Francisco Madero had in turn been set aside by his own enforcer Victoriano Huerta. It is interesting to speculate what Theodore Roosevelt would have done with the situation. Wilson, newly arrived in the White House, refused to recognise Huerta's government, on the principled but misguided grounds that Mexico did not seem to be following the paths of constitutional democracy. Business interests in the US were appalled, fearing that their investments were threatened by instability south of the border. In the face of the American ambassador Henry Lane Wilson's strong support for the charismatic and hard-drinking Huerta, Wilson sent his own emissaries, bypassing Bryan's State Department. William Bayard Hale was despatched on a fact-finding mission (and found Huerta to be exactly as the ambassador had said); Robert Lind was sent – empirical turning into evangelical – to convert Mexico to democracy, broker a cease-fire and persuade Huerta to step aside. Properly run elections and an agreement to abide by the result would guarantee American friendship and restore hemispheric equilibrium.

The Princeton trustees had suavely declined Wilson's proposals in 1910. Huerta merely threw these later ones back in his face. For a man who seemed to carry all before him at home, this was a shock. Wilson agonised over a crisis which seemed to be deepening with the emergence of an armed opposition, led by Madero's supporter Venustiano Carranza and his promising-sounding Constitutionalists, and in the rural South by Emiliano Zapata. He also feared that the UK and Germany, not yet at war with one another, might defend their interests in Mexico by force, a violation of the Monroe Doctrine. Wilson reversed Taft's embargo on arms sales to the Constitutionalists. In April 1914, he was obliged to put American forces on stand-by when one of Huerta's officers arrested American sailors who had gone ashore at Tampico and misbehaved. Right was on the Mexicans' side, but Wilson treated the matter as an opportunity to undermine Huerta. He asked Congress to authorise military action, but took the initiative in advance of a reply when it was discovered that a German ship was about to dock at Vera Cruz with weapons for the provisional government. There were 90 American casualties in the attack on Vera Cruz, 19 of them fatal; the Mexicans suffered 300, of which a third were killed. Wilson had acted in a manner more typically associated with his presidential rival and brought down on his own head and on his country's Latin American interests the vituperation of the continent the US was pledged to protect. His willingness to accept the mediation of Argentina, Brazil and Chile (the so-called 'ABC' solution) had more to do with repairing diplomatic rents and tears than with compromise; Wilson remained committed to the ousting of Huerta.

That was achieved in July 1914, with the Constitutionalist forces providing the anvil, Zapata the hammer, and American weapons the firepower. With absolute consistency, Wilson pointed out that Carranza's assumption of the presidency was achieved with reference to the popular will. The successes of Constitutionalist general Francisco 'Pancho' Villa, led Wilson briefly to believe that he might have discovered an alternative leader, but by the end of 1915 he was obliged to recognise Carranza, if only grudgingly and by default. Villa not unexpectedly believed himself betrayed and turned on Americans, killing a group of mining engineers in Sonora and later, in January 1916, crossing the border and attacking Columbus, New Mexico, leaving behind 17 American dead. Wilson sent General John Pershing after him, and Carranza felt obliged to resist the invader. After Pershing's 'Punitive Expedition', the whole thing quietened down but was never quite resolved.

The Mexican adventure swallowed up the journalist and short-story writer Ambrose Bierce, who disappeared there sometime in 1914. Best known for his darkly cynical re-definitions of cherished concepts, published as *The Cynic's Word Book* and *The Devil's Dictionary,* Bierce delivered a bleakly prescient observation shortly before he vanished: 'PEACE, *n.* In international affairs, a period of cheating between two periods of fighting.'[3] Almost exactly a century later, that remains the consensus view of the Paris settlement. For the moment, Bierce's dim view of alliances as a kind of higher larceny must have chimed strongly with Wilson, as it had would have done with American presidents back to Washington.

The Mexican adventure swallowed up some of Wilson's self-possession, too. Real-world politics were not always susceptible to providence or reason. The experience did, though, demonstrate to him how freely a president could work in similar situations, even with a frankly pacifist secretary of state in place. He intervened in both Haiti and the Dominican Republic when disturbances there threatened the

THE MONROE DOCTRINE

In 1822, France and Spain seemed on the brink of alliance against the newly-established republics in South America. Britain and the US were concerned about trade arrangements. The British prime minister George Canning proposed a counter-alliance, but influential opinion in America warned against any appearance of simply joining a British plan. On 2 December 1823, in his seventh State of the Union address, US President James Monroe declared that henceforward all of the Americas would be closed to further European colonisation and that any intervention in the hemisphere would be regarded as a threat to American security.

Though the 'Monroe Doctrine', as it became known was born out of a fear of colonialism, it was later used, under the terms of the so-called 'Roosevelt Corollary' and subsequent developments, to justify American intervention in Latin America where political or economic instability threatened, making the United States a 'hemispheric policeman'. In 1928 the so-called 'Clark Memorandum' stated that America's sovereignty and freedom of action no longer required the Monroe Doctrine, though it was subsequently evoked by John Foster Dulles, John F Kennedy and Ronald Reagan.

economic equilibrium of the Caribbean basin, an explicit exercise of Roosevelt's 'Corollary' to the Monroe Doctrine giving America *de facto* police status in the region, but Wilson also went against Roosevelt's bullish co-option of the Panama Canal as an American interest – TR's trip to view its construction was the first overseas trip by an incumbent president; Wilson's long sojourn in Paris was the next – but unilaterally and against pressure from within his own party suspending toll exemptions for American shipping using the canal. The decision pleased the British, who regarded the world's oceans and waterways as spheres of special interest, and like his parallel decision to cancel a large loan to China, ratified by Taft, it underlined Wilson's conviction that principle needed to be applied disinterestedly and not in the interests of 'dollar diplomacy'.

NORWAY
Kristiania
North Sea
UNITED KINGDOM
Dublin
DENMARK
Copenhagen
NETHERLANDS
Amsterdam
London
Brussels
BELGIUM
GERMAN EMPIRE
LUXEMBOURG
Paris
FRANCE
SWITZERLAND
AUSTRIA
Milan
Trieste
Istria
Pala
ITALY
PORTUGAL
Madrid
Lisbon
SPAIN
Rome
SPANISH MOROCCO
Mediterranean Sea
MOROCCO
ALGERIA
TUNISIA
0 500 kilometres

Europe 1914
Petrograd (St Petersburg)
Riga
Moscow
Vilna
Königsberg
RUSSIAN EMPIRE
Warsaw
Brest-Litovsk
Kiev
udapest
RY
Odessa
ROMANIA
Bucharest
Belgrade
Black Sea
SERBIA
BULGARIA
Sofia
Constantinople
NIA
GREECE
OTTOMAN EMPIRE
Athens

Finance, and its political and diplomatic ramifications, became an issue right at the start of the European war. The French, whose economy was still recovering from the *débacle* of 1870, immediately applied to US bankers for help in selling bonds. Bryan was no supporter of the banks and as a pacifist was disinclined to become involved in a foreign war; he regarded money as the most insidious contraband of all. Wilson was initially inclined to agree, but the wily French made it clear that any American credits would be used to buy American goods. In 1914, America was still in a recession, arguably sharpened by Wilson's fiscal reforms which were taking some time to bed in, and any opportunity for profitable overseas trade was welcome. It was not long before the United States was making outright loans to belligerent governments. German-American interests – the insidious 'hyphenates' – offered support to the Central Powers, Swedes tended to be sympathetic to Germany and the powerful Jewish lobby longed for the destruction of Tsarist Russia, but by 1916 ten times as much American money was going to the Allies, and particularly to the United Kingdom. This was partly in line with the realities of trade – Germany and the Austro-Hungarian Empire were effectively blockaded; British sea power and a huge merchant marine meant that, even after the submarine campaign escalated, the Allies were not – but if it looks like *de facto* support for one side over another, it was. Even so, Wilson's hand was stayed a little by friction with Britain over specific violations of international law, such as a strict embargo on trade with Germany, and lesser, but symbolic, issues such as the mining of the North Sea, which meant that British pilots were required for safe navigation. Whether Wilson accepted the situation without undue protest because his instincts – what Spring-Rice described to Sir Edward Grey as an 'understanding heart' – were with the United Kingdom, or simply because British control of the high seas suited the US for the time being is hard to judge.[4]

In effect, the *wide and universal forces of mankind* spoke English and French. Wilson was keenly aware of other accents and other sympathies in the complex harmony of American life, but he was also convinced that American interests, American philosophies and principles were best served by an Allied victory, a view shared by most of his cabinet, with Bryan the only significant dissenter. Wilson's apparent commitment to neutrality, on which he won the 1916 election, was a staying action. His subsequent about-turn was more perceived than actual. If pressed, Wilson might well have conceded that American involvement was inevitable, but he was aware that the United States was, in practical terms, unprepared. A Jeffersonian suspicion of large standing armies meant that the American military was significantly under strength – and already deployed in the festering conflict in Mexico – and there was a prevailing, though largely subliminal belief that war-mongering, and the diplomatic subterfuge and spying that went with it, was an atavistic expression of the feudal and monarchical cultures of Europe, where high-density populations and scarce free land inevitably led to conflict. America, with her wide open spaces, libertarian philosophy and democratic government, was believed to have evolved beyond or to have transcended such dark indignities. Not only did America not have a large army or navy (certainly in comparison to the Royal Navy), she did not have a fully professional foreign service or intelligence-gathering network. Another reason for Wilson's delaying was that he simply did not know enough about the situation in Europe, and that what he knew was coloured and overdetermined by an experience of English rural life and high-minded English philosophy.

Other factors were at work. The actual course of the war was a surprise to the belligerents, who had expected relatively quick and devastating victories and who had found themselves locked in stalemate instead. This might have been less of a surprise to a man who had witnessed – albeit in childhood, and at a certain distance – the first truly industrialised war in history and one in which prolonged stalemate, human attrition and devastating losses were documented in detail both by journalists and by a civil population caught up in conflict as never before. The impact of the Civil War is rarely adduced as a factor in Wilson's thinking, but it is undoubtedly an important one.

There is no such thing as a man being too proud to fight. There is such a thing a nation being so right that it does not need to convince others by force that it is right.
WOODROW WILSON

In his marrow, Wilson wanted peace. He shrank from violence – his famous assertion that a country, like a man, could be too proud to fight was a direct echo of his mother's horror of vulgar fisticuffs – and in the crucial spring and summer of 1915, when American lives began to be lost at sea, he was a man euphorically in love, wooing Edith Bolling Galt with the ardour of a man half his almost-60 years.[5] Men in love are less inclined to vote for war. Wilson was conflicted, though, to the extent that not only pragmatism dictated some level of involvement, so too did his principled belief that if the United States wished to become a player on the world stage, she could not entirely avoid bloody 'entanglements'. There remained the hope that America might affect the outcome without military intervention, either by the economic route, or else as peace-broker. By 1916, more than 10 per cent of American output was going overseas, and even if the overwhelmingly

THE LEAGUE TO ENFORCE PEACE

The League to Enforce Peace (LTEP) was a significant forerunner in the United States of the League of Nations idea. Founded at a conference at Independence Hall in Philadelphia on 17 June 1915, the LTEP advocated the establishment of a world court and a process of mandatory conciliation. Its co-chairman was ex-president William Howard Taft, Wilson's Republican predecessor in the White House and a former Secretary of War under Theodore Roosevelt, during which time he had actively promoted both the idea of 'dollar diplomacy', later practised during his administration, and the idea of international arbitration for potentially lethal disputes. Taft was appointed to a chair in law and legal history at Yale Law School on leaving the White House, and was subsequently (1921–30) the Chief Justice of the United States. Other prominent members included Hamilton Holt, a temperance reformer and supporter of minority rights, who compiled a collection of immigrant memoirs, *The Life Stories of Undistinguished Americans, as Told by Themselves,* Harvard president A Lawrence Lowell and Theodore Marburg, who had been the American envoy to Belgium from 1912 to the beginning of the First World War.

Wilson was ambivalent about the LTEP's work, and particularly Taft's notion that a fixed global constitution – a version of 'world government' based on the American model would work. He evaded an undertaking to address the LTEP until May 1916, when he required a platform to persuade the Allies to accept the US as a peace-broker. In March 1918, he met with Taft and Lowell in a bid to persuade them not to publish an alternative plan for a League of Nations that might compete with his own and confuse or divide public opinion.

Though Taft's own views bordered on pacifism, he actively supported conscription when the US entered the war in 1917 and warned of the dangers of a 'finicky' war which might simply prolong the conflict. The organisation's mostly conservative, Republican and pro-Ally membership also insisted that its main function was not to bring to an end the European war but to guard against future hostilities. These attitudes, coupled with the LTEP's emphasis on economic and military 'enforcement', alienated much potential support among anti-war and pacifist groups and its influence declined rapidly, though it continued to hold conventions and assemblies, most critically in February 1919, at the time the League of Nations Covenant was first presented in Paris. The League to Enforce Peace was disbanded in 1921.

Other influential American anti-war organisations of the time included the Women's Peace Party, established by Jane Addams, founder of the Hull House settlement and, like Wilson, a Nobel Peace Prize winner.

major proportion of vital steel production – which was more than double that of the European powers put together – was being used for domestic projects, it was still potentially vital to a prolonged Allied war effort. On the peace front, Colonel House was despatched to Europe in the summer of 1914 in an effort to defuse the crisis. Ironically, it was House who two years later tried to dissuade Wilson from sending a tough letter to the warring powers asking for a cease-fire, and it was House to whom Wilson deferred when drafting a speech eventually given in May 1916 to the League to Enforce Peace in order that it might be interpreted as both neutral – or even notionally pacifist – and pro-Ally. Wilson continued to hope for a quick and peaceful solution, all the while preparing for war.

The main stages in this were not overtly military. In 1915, with Allied losses at sea already significant, Wilson tried to push through McAdoo's measure to create a strong merchant marine by setting up a government corporation to purchase ships. There were concerns that purchasing interned German ships would be a violation of neutrality and the measure was defeated, reminding Wilson that he no longer had easy Congressional momentum. It was not until the following year that he managed to secure the establishment of a Shipping Board, whose existence eventually eased the transport of American servicemen to France. In a tiny historical irony, the liner *George Washington* that transported Wilson to France in 1918 was a captured German vessel.

Wilson's cleverest political strategy was to declare himself uninterested in the causes or the objects of the war. At an informal diplomatic level, he was able to allow House to agree with British ministers on specific Allied war aims, while publicly he could declare that the desire for peace must override any merely national goal. In the same way, suggesting that the underlying cause of war was an almost genetic European propensity for secret alliances, allowed him to avoid making any public condemnation of German aggression. However, at the same time, Wilson tried to win over public opinion to the Allied cause by propagating atrocity stories. The symbolic rape of Belgium was quickly accompanied in American minds by the literal violation of Belgian nuns, the bayoneting of babies, shooting of prisoners, burning of churches and hospitals and all the other 'horrors of war' bequeathed to the Western imagination by narratives of the Thirty Years War and the etchings of Francisco Goya. These are not far-fetched analogies. There is something darkly pre-modern to many of the stories circulated in the US about German crimes, a certain literariness of cast that suggests many of these stories were confected rather than reported, as well as a second-hand vagueness that is now recognised as the defining characteristic of that thoroughly modern phenomenon, the urban legend.

In the spring of 1915, though, in the midst of personal happiness, Wilson was forced to confront an act that could not be rendered down into moral abstractions. In February of that year, Germany had declared a war zone round British waters and had warned that all shipping entering it would be in jeopardy of attack. It has already been stated that at this time very few Americans indeed actually travelled abroad. Almost more significant, though, was the failure to believe that the German navy would attack unarmed merchant ships. If the sinking of the *Titanic* in 1912 put a heavy caesura in Victorian hubris, suggesting that industrial might was less mighty than cold, implacable nature, the torpedoing of the *Lusitania*, a comparably iconic vessel, off the coast of Ireland on 7 May 1915, was a reminder that behind all the carefully elaborated and wilfully believed tales of horror from Europe there was also real and irreducible evil, wearing German uniforms and sailing under a German flag. The presence of 128 mostly wealthy American names among the casualties has tended to deflect the recognition that 1,200 souls perished on the ship. The fact that no newsreel captured the event did not make it less searingly emotive than the World Trade Center attacks of 11 September 2001. The impact was comparable.

As on 9/11, those of a warlike tendency immediately called for war. Theodore Roosevelt deemed some decisive response a matter of pride, speaking as he often did for an East Coast constituency that was increasingly and vocally pro-Ally. In the Midwest, far from the sea and ships, but absolutely the heart of the new Democratic power and with a strong German-American demographic, there was no such feeling. In the South-West, inevitably, there was more concern about the situation in Mexico, and when Wilson ran in 1916 on the slogan 'He kept us out of the war', many in that region would have interpreted that as meaning a full-scale conflict across the Rio Grande rather than in Europe. For the moment, Wilson attempted to broker a position mid-way between Roosevelt's aggression and Bryan's pacifism.

Roosevelt remained a key figure in American electoral politics. When he declined to stand again for the Progressives and throw in his hand with Charles Evans Hughes, former Republican governor of New York state and former Supreme Court judge, the Bull Moose Party promptly fell apart and disbanded. In the 1916 campaign Wilson could comfortably stand on his record and on the undivided loyalty of the Democratic Party. In addition, he could again rely on a compromised opposition. With Roosevelt again exerting his outsize personality in the Republican Party, it was inevitable that

Hughes, always an advocate of preparedness, should be identified as the pro-war candidate. His only significant grounds for criticising Wilson were the allegedly damaging impact of a limited working day on business interests and the muddle and subterfuge of his handling of the Mexican situation. In practice, Wilson concentrated his attacks on Roosevelt and largely ignored Hughes, allegedly commenting that it was bad form to attack a man who was intent on committing suicide. Once again, Wilson was proved correct. While campaigning in California, Hughes snubbed the powerful Republican governor Hiram W Johnson, who withdrew critical support.

The objective situation reinforced Wilson's position of non-intervention. Relations with Britain were already strained. As early as the autumn of 1914, Robert Lansing, future Secretary of State but then a legal advisor in the State Department, had drafted a protest against the seizing of 'contraband' by the British navy. After the *Lusitania* sinking, Lansing was moved to make the laconic point that there was a clear moral distinction between destruction of property and destruction of human life; Lansing was, however, also involved in covering up the fact that the liner had been carrying American arms (whether this squared or not with his own position of 'benevolent neutrality' can only be judged) and it was this clandestine activity, as well as Wilson's strong protest to the Germans, that led to Bryan's resignation and replacement by Lansing. The 'legitimacy' of the liner as a military target has been much discussed. The suggestion that a second, devastating explosion on the ship was caused by American munitions can be discounted (though she was carrying small-arms) and it is a matter of fact that, classed as a naval auxiliary, the ship was a legitimate target according to the rules of engagement.

Wilson's carefully-phrased protest, which hinted at but did

not specify potential reprisals, led to the suspension of unrestricted submarine warfare, not so much a public relations coup, as a stroke of political luck – not much more – that bought him time. He seemed to be having less luck with the Allies and in the summer of 1916 relations were exceedingly strained. Wilson was furious that Balfour and Clemenceau rebuffed him as a peace-broker, even as they set about framing principles of economic co-operation *after* a war that seemed at the time – the bloody stalemate on the Somme played out in the background – far from easily winnable and not set to end soon. Wilson's Irish background meant that he shared much of the Irish-American community's horror at Britain's bloody suppression of the Easter Rising, and the subsequent execution of its leaders, though after the war he seemed disinclined to extend the principle of 'self-determination' to Irish Republicans. The blacklisting of American firms believed to be dealing with the enemy and the interception of American mail – the Old World serpent reverting to stealthy type – infuriated Wilson so much that he seriously considered the suspension of aid and exports to the Allies. He would have met stiff opposition in Congress, and the remark – to House – may have been nothing more than an outburst of frustration. (One suspects that this was one of House's key roles, as a semi-official confidant and safety-valve, a role that became less valuable, or less valued, as events unfolded.)

Rhetoric aside, Wilson went into the 1916 election only slightly less likely than a year earlier to go to war, still juggling strong response to German aggression with a genuine desire to forestall actual intervention. He also went into it with only a slim expectation of winning. So unsure was he of a mandate that he told Lansing of his plan to resign immediately on defeat but having appointed Hughes Secretary of

State first, which under the existing constitutional arrangement would have meant that Hughes became president at once rather than waiting for a formal hand-over and inaugural in March 1917. There is a famous story that a newspaperman phoned Hughes' hotel on the morning of 8 November 1916 to be told 'the President is sleeping'. The journalist suggested that the aide wake him up and tell him that he wasn't president any more. During the night, against the odds and at least partly thanks to Hughes' gaffe in California, Wilson had done the improbable, winning re-election by carrying 30 states and 49 per cent of the popular vote. He even failed to win his home state.

Given that both candidates had a strong progressive record, what had swayed the result for Wilson was the peace issue. Wilson was paradoxically by this time becoming convinced that the main questions about American military intervention were not whether and why but when and how much. At the end of 1915, a year to the day before the election, Wilson was warning Americans that preparedness was essential; ironically, the fact that military activity continued in Haiti and Mexico, and would for the next six months in Mexico and the Dominican Republic, reconciled many Americans to military action, by demonstrating the efficacy of military action towards specifically American ends. Although Wilson had sent a second aggressive note to Germany after the *Lusitania* sinking (aggressive but notably vague about consequences), the State Department was still relatively slow in response and unmanouevrable. The initiative was being taken by House and on the spot in Europe, where he was acting as a semi-official ambassador and go-between. Some of the differences in approach between House and Lansing, which came to a head later, were undoubtedly innate, but working as he was in the corridors of a state already at war and among highly and subtly persuasive men, House became susceptible. Where Lansing always seemed to feel that diplomatic overtures or initiatives like the removal of armament from American merchantmen to facilitate stop-and-search might defuse the situation, House saw American involvement as inevitable and in the interests of a grand liberal vision; in that respect, House was much closer to the President, who increasingly considered Lansing to be over-fussy with detail and unwilling to match clear statement of objectives with decisive action. However, Wilson probably over-estimated the unwillingness of the American people to go to war or to take a tough stand against Germany, and to this degree House and Lansing had a clearer understanding of the domestic situation. Through his discussions with the British Foreign Secretary Sir Edward Grey, House was increasingly persuaded of the need for an urgent and positive commitment by the United States to the Allied cause, and a commitment that went beyond academic settlement of matter of international law; in this regard, Colonel House played the idealistic cowboy, while Wilson could scarcely shrug off the gown of a professor of jurisprudence. House and Grey worked on their memorandum in 1916 and sent back the suggestion that, in order to guarantee world peace and security, American might consider joining

SIR EDWARD GREY (1862–1933)
Sir Edward Grey – subsequently Viscount Grey of Fallodon, under which name he was known as a distinguished ornithologist – became foreign secretary in the Liberal government in 1905 and held the post for 11 years, a record which still stands. During the war, Grey was instrumental in securing Italy's entry through the Treaty of London, and kept in close contact with the Americans through Cecil Spring-Rice. Also during 1915, he discussed an American role as a peace broker with Colonel House, on the basis of American stewardship of a league of nations, which Grey described as a 'pearl of great price'.[6]

and playing a key role in a great League of Nations. Like so many of Wilson's ideas and commitments, this one was of British origin as well.

ooooo

Bryan's departure had infuriated Wilson – *I sincerely deplore it*, he said in a markedly unfriendly reply to the resignation letter – not so much because it made any fundamental difference to a logic of thinking and events that was moving inexorably in the direction advocated by House, but because it suggested a divided administration and because it handed the anti-war lobby an immediate champion in the time-honoured form of 'the Great Commoner'.[7] He might have prevented the split had he not been in such a volatile frame of mind at the time.

Wilson had met Edith Bolling Galt, whose vivacious widowhood contrasted sharply with his own emotional doldrums after Ellen's death, through Dr Grayson, who seems to have engineered an encounter between his employer and his lady friend almost as kind of therapy for the emotionally ailing president. Wilson himself suggested that his infamous comment about a country being too proud to fight was made off-the-cuff in Philadelphia while he was thinking about Edith back in Washington. She was, in essence, very much like himself, a Virginian reshaped by the north, and the only seeming obstacle to their marriage was, on the cusp of the election year, whether the American people would consider it over-hasty. Wilson and Edith made their vows on 18 December 1915.

Following the sinking of the *Lusitania*, the German admiralty sent a secret directive to U-boat commanders not to attack ships likely to be carrying passengers. On 19 August 19, however, the *Arabic* was sunk; two of the 48 dead were Americans. In order to defuse the situation, and to the fury of his government, the German ambassador Johan Bernstorff revealed the secret order, implying that the commander who had torpedoed the *Arabic* was either flouting the directive or else had simply misidentified his target. Given the primitive technology of the time, such mistakes were almost inevitable. Matters came to a head with the sinking in March 1916 of the French-registered *Sussex* in the English Channel, with the loss of 80 lives, including the composer Eugene Granados and his wife. Despite Germany's attempt to pass off the incident as the work of a British mine, Wilson was pressed hard by both House and Lansing to take a tough stand. Wilson was already campaigning for re-election and he knew that peace was becoming a key issue for American voters, whose attitudes were hardening as a result of pro-war propaganda and by a number of acts of sabotage on American soil, most notably the fire-bombing and subsequent explosion of the Black Tom munitions dump in New Jersey; the detonation was heard in Philadelphia and showered the Statue of Liberty across the bay with debris. Wilson recognised that such acts and non-fatal injury to four Americans on the *Sussex* were not a *casus belli* in the way the *Lusitania* sinking might have been, he once again temporised. Concentrating in his speech to both houses of Congress the illegality and immorality of German actions and threatening to sever diplomatic relations if there were any repetition.

The Kaiser's government could read – and send – diplomatic code very well. The German admiralty agreed to observe the rules of warfare in dealing with merchant ships, but demanded in return that America put pressure on Britain to ease the naval blockade that was strangling the Central Powers. It was, as Lansing and others recognised, a highly conditional concession; the Germans were aware that only Wilson could exert any leverage on the Allies, but also that they could not afford, in the military situation then prevailing, to push him into a declaration of war. Wilson in turn knew that he had now handed some of the initiative to Germany. He also knew that war could only be ratified with the agreement of Congress, so his freedoms were limited. After November 1916, this mattered less, because as a second-term president Wilson was no longer constrained by political interests. It was, however, the deepest flaw of the memorandum prepared by House and Grey in early 1916, that it called for American participation in a peace conference with the rider that, should the conference fail to bring about a cessation of hostilities, American would enter the war on the Allied side. Fully conscious that such a promise could not reliably be delivered, Wilson insisted on adding the word 'probably', which effectively holed the memorandum below the water-line.

First of all, it must be a peace without victory. Victory would mean peace forced upon the loser, a victor's terms imposed upon the vanquished. It would be accepted in humiliation, under duress, at an intolerable sacrifice, and would leave a sting, a resentment, a bitter memory upon which terms of peace would rest, not permanently, but only as upon quicksand.
WOODROW WILSON

Once re-elected, Wilson began to cast himself more unilaterally in the role of peace-broker. On 18 December 1916, his and Edith's first wedding anniversary, he asked the belligerents to state the terms on which they might make peace. If

Wilson expected clear statement, he received none. The question may have been partly rhetorical, allowing him to return to some of the ideas set out in his address to the League to Enforce Peace six months earlier. A month later, Wilson addressed the Senate and made his famous call for *a peace without victory*, dashing off a grimly prescient sketch of the repercussions – humiliation, duress, resentment, bitterness – of an imposed peace.[8] Wilson was only too well aware that the European nations had already endured almost 30 months of unprecedented destruction and that calls for magnanimity and further sacrifice might sound hollow coming from a large nation that had so far kept out of war. Wilson, though, made firm connections between peace-without-victory, disarmament, freedom of the seas, a wholesale extension of the principle of government by popular consent (this in keeping with his later insistence that the war was fought against the Kaiser and the Prussian military class rather than against the German people), and, above, all the establishment of an international League of Peace that would replace the pattern of rival alliances he considered to be behind the war and what in another context entirely he might have described as the 'literary theory' of the balance of power with a community of power.

The speech was well received in the Senate and heralded publicly as a triumph of American moral principle, even though premised on the still somewhat un-American notion of international commitment. The nature of that commitment would depend largely on external events, but on 2 April 1917 Wilson stood before Congress and, after laying out the various stages in his attempt to keep American out of the war, asserted that 'the right is more precious than peace' and asked both houses to ratify a declaration of war.[9]

Having committed himself to the principle of peace without victory, Wilson was obliged to commit himself and his country to a war without self-interested war aims (*We have no selfish ends to serve*), and to a war with no other object than the elimination of war. For some of his listeners, this was buckling on one item of moral armour too many. *The world must be made safe for democracy* is resounding enough for its slight oddity to go unnoted. It is as if the genetic principle of democracy – the gene or meme of American philosophy and practice – is more important than *the world*, which is required to conform and plant peace only *upon the tested foundations of political liberty.*[10]

It was a speech Wilson had long resisted making, and had held back even as events overtook any uncertainties he may have retained. The early months of 1917 saw events in a fateful lockstep. Italy was all but out of the picture, which relieved pressure on the Central Powers more generally, but more significantly, ten days after Wilson's second inaugural, the Russian Tsar abdicated. Germany was now fighting on one front only, a situation that put immense strain on Allied resistance on the Western Front – Britain was nearly bankrupt; morale in the decimated French army had almost collapsed – and raised the spectre of a replenished German army breaking the deadlock and pushing on to Paris. The republican – not yet Bolshevik – victory also removed a squeamish obstacle for Wilson, who felt that while Tsarist Russia was one of the Allies, the United States could hardly claim to be making the world safe for democracy. In fact, he completely misread the new Russian government's position as a simulacrum of American liberalism; like Lloyd George, but unlike Clemenceau, who thought the Bolsheviks were German patsies and likened the Bolshevik Revolution to the

Terror which overtook the revolution of 1789, Wilson was originally optimistic about Russia's new rulers and about the sweeping away of the old order, but he was repelled by their methods and his confidence that Europe could withstand the creep of Communist ideas eroded as events unfolded in 1918 and 1919.

For the moment, with the situation in the East changing, the German command was increasingly aware that American involvement, and above all its timing, would be the decisive factor in the war. With some perversity, though there now seems no doubt that the document was genuine, the government set about trying to ensure that the United States would also have to fight on more than one front. British – significantly – cryptanalysts in Naval Intelligence Division 25 (known as 'Room 40') intercepted a telegram from German foreign minister Arthur Zimmermann to the embassy in Mexico proposing an alliance between Germany, Mexico and Japan against the United States, with a promise to help restore Arizona, New Mexico and Texas to Mexican control. The action seems so pointlessly provocative that the Zimmermann Telegram has been dismissed as a forgery. In point of fact, Germany was by this time largely convinced of imminent American involvement and was merely trying to rein back a runaway horse. Such was the doublethink of politics in these months that on the same day the German ambassador in Washington delivered the announcement that would ultimately propel America into the conflict, he was still also warmly acknowledging Wilson's calls for a peace conference but continuing to press his country's inability in the face of Allied calls for the destruction and dismantlement of the Central Powers, to do anything less than fight on for victory and with whatever means available. Diplomatic relations between the countries were severed on 3 February, four days after Germany announced the resumption of unrestricted submarine warfare – which this time *meant* unrestricted: all vessels, under whatever flag, merchant as well as naval – in the seas round the British Isles. There had been an interim suggestion that a renewed campaign against naval ships and armed merchantmen only might be sufficient or might at least keep America out of the war. But the political initiative was firmly in the hands of those, like Ludendorff and Hindenburg who believed that a ruthless submarine campaign might effect the defeat of Britain before American troops arrived in the field.

It was one of the great gambles of modern political history, and its failure had global consequences. Wilson had been playing golf on the morning of 31 January and learned about the German decision from an Associated Press despatch when he returned to the White House. Lansing was asked to prepare a note breaking off relations. Colonel House, to whom Wilson had remarked the previous November that the American people would not wish to go to war over a few sunken ships, arrived the following day with a personal note to Wilson from Chancellor Bethmann-Hollweg (soon to fall from grace as the hardliners, or the desperate rearguard, took over), but still Wilson seemed unwilling to take the fatal step and for once was swayed by the views of 16 Democratic senators at a hastily convened meeting (that is why no Republicans were present) in the Capitol. Wilson was now under pressure to secure armed protection for American merchantmen. On 26 February, while he was addressing Congress, news arrived that the British-registered Cunard liner *Laconia* had been sunk, with American casualties. On 18 March, Washington received news that three American vessels had been sunk, including the tanker *Illinois,* with loss of life. The 'irony of fate' was sealed. Because American soil had not been invaded, because the ocean lay in between, because the step about to be taken was unprecedented as well as enormous in scale, and because the American Constitution provides for due democratic process, there was no echo of the European rush to battle in August 1914. Wilson delivered his War Address on 2 April. Four days later, on 6 April 1917, America declared war on Germany only; Wilson had no quarrel with the Austro-Hungarian Empire, other than that it was a bloated and repressive anachronism; he even had doubts that the dismantling or territorial restriction of Germany was a good thing. His opponents were now divided between those who felt the decision overdue and who would have gone to war the moment the first American drop of blood was spilt or the first American sank beneath the waves – and who certainly regarded the *Lusitania* atrocity as sufficient provocation – and those who saw in it a betrayal of the very spirit Wilson had invoked, of American exceptionalism, and of the Founding Fathers themselves. Whatever the case, the United States would be at war for the next 19 months.

4

Force without stint or limit

Woodrow Wilson was determined to take charge of the peace but was content to leave the conduct of the war to others: this conventional view requires some adjustment, because while Wilson took little active part in strategy planning and even in wartime diplomacy, he made very significant efforts to align American society behind the military, significantly reshaping both in the process. Unlike in 1941, American soil had not been attacked, and though the war resolution passed both houses of Congress comfortably, the fact of six dissenting senators and 50 congressmen left support for declaration of war far short of unanimous, with significant resistance in the Midwest where the proportion of German-American voters was highest. Wilson also lost support in the South, though here it may have been direct memories of the horrors of trench warfare – as much a feature of the American Civil War as of the Western Front – that swayed feelings.

Wilson was, as ever, convinced that politics was first and foremost a hearts-and-minds business. In April 1917, he established the Committee on Public Information (CPI), under the chairmanship of the 'muckraking' journalist George Creel (hence 'Creel Committee') and with Robert Lansing and Secretaries of War and the Navy, Newman D Baker and Josephus Daniels as members. An ostensibly independent body, its purpose was to snuff out anti-war feeling and in large measure to reassure blue-collar Germans, both industrial and agricultural, that the fight was specifically against a repressive Kaiser (*The Beast of Berlin* in one CPI film title), his Hohenzollern dynasty and the aristocratic martial class that propped up his reign, and not against the German people themselves. Wilson himself shifted his position on the causes of the war: from arguing that its roots lay in relative abstractions such as 'militarism' and 'nationalism' or to atavistic forces at work in the Old World, he laid blame squarely at Germany's door. Despite the work of illustrators Charles Dana Gibson and Louis D Fancher, and the writing of Ray Stannard Baker, a future Wilson biographer, the Committee's work was crude, relying largely on out-of-context testimony about German 'atrocities' and often pure fiction. Creel himself regarded – or presented – his work as positive rather than negative, referring to the CPI's work as the grandest adventure in advertising and salesmanship and giving 'propaganda' a positive spin as the 'propagation of faith'. This may have been the kind of talk that attracted Wilson, and Wilson himself was the CPI's most successful branding. The President's personality and record were talked up by the so-called 'Four Minute Men' who gave nearly three quarters of a million short morale speeches round the country between mid-1917 and mid-1918. Wilson's image and words were also widely distributed in Europe, stoking up the atmosphere of almost hysterical reverence that initially greeted him in France and Italy before the formal start of the Peace Conference.

Wilson took more strenuous legislative measures to reach

the same ends, introducing an Espionage Act in 1917 and a more stringent Sedition Act in 1918. The veteran socialist Eugene Debs was jailed for his opposition to the war. A delegation of socialists bound for a peace conference in Stockholm was barred from attending. Members of the American Protective League, essentially a body of government-sanctioned vigilantes, carried out warrantless searches, phone-taps, and on occasion humiliating assaults on anyone suspected of pro-German sympathies or leftist leanings. To the dismay of Randolph Bourne, many on the liberal left like Walter Lippmann and Edward Bernays remained close to a wartime administration that was now accelerating a highly progressive fiscal policy, deriving most of its revenue from income tax rather than the tariff and targeting the better-off in the process. Wilson, though, was also minded to go soft on defaulting businessmen under investigation for pre-war wrong-doing. With the tacit consent of the War Industries Board, a neat rebranding of the Federal Trade Commission, industry was allowed to benefit relatively unchecked from a spiralling war economy.

Not much more than an hour after signing the war resolution in the lobby of the White House, Wilson and his cabinet were discussing mobilisation, a role which ultimately fell to future Army Chief of Staff General Tasker H Bliss (1853–1930), who had reorganised the American army in 1902, on the orders of Secretary of War Elihu Root. Most contingencies were already in place, though Wilson had been obliged to drop his 1916 plan for a 'Continental Army' of half a million reservists, a decision that forced the resignation of Secretary of War Lindley M Garrison, and his replacement by Baker. The passing of the National Defense Act in 1916, one of the most important pieces of legislation in modern

American history, had provided for federal first call on all state guards and militias in the event of national emergency and paved the way for conscription of all men between the ages of 18 and 45, an unprecedently sweeping measure. For all Wilson's resistance to actual war, it had seemed the only possible one to many of his advisers for some time. (And to some of his opponents: Theodore Roosevelt was an early visitor to the White House, unexpectedly charming the President, though not ultimately convincing him with the suggestion of a volunteer division for France, led by TR himself.) The declaration of war was not prompted by a sneak attack, and was determined by a fine balance of circumstance and spin. Conscription was inevitable and *de facto* nationalisation of the rail network advisable to speed movement of men across the continent, though this step was only taken when problems of co-ordination began to emerge. Fuel and food supply were similarly handed over to federal administration and monitoring. A Selective Service Act was signed in May 1917, but government control of the railways was not secured until December by which time American deployment was moving towards its impressive maximum of 10,000 men per day and a total of four million men in arms.

Counterfactual history – the same speculative discipline that cast Wilson as president of the Confederacy – asks what would have happened if America had not entered the war. Some New Left historians have argued that by intervening militarily rather than merely continuing to provide financial aid, America brought about the very end Wilson had seemed determined to prevent – the destruction, humiliation and at least partial dismantlement of Germany – and in the end established a habit of military engagement overseas that led inexorably on through Korea, Vietnam and the Gulf, as well as a dozen other smaller police actions, American backed and overturned coups. According to this logic, the opposing armies were so near exhaustion that the war would almost certainly have petered out of its own accord sometime in 1918 or 1919, allowing Wilson to broker some version of 'peace without victory' as a disinterested onlooker. With hindsight, it is even possible to argue that the influenza epidemic might have halted the fighting as the two sides discovered that there was a force at work in the world even more powerful than themselves.

Such a model requires a Tsar on the throne and a continuing struggle on the Eastern Front. Stiffened by divisions from the East, Ludendorff's spring 1918 offensive very nearly overran the Allies in the West. A more interesting question than the counterfactual one is what impact American military intervention *did* make in France. The received view is that it was small in strictly military terms but significant overall, and there is no pressing need to overturn this interpretation beyond adding that what made American presence on the Western Front so valuable was not the actual presence of troops but the promise of an almost inexhaustible flow of men and materiel from the world's fastest-growing industrial power. America's entry into the war was an effective warrant of eventual victory.

> **'From a military point of view America is as nothing.'**
> COUNT EDUARD VON CAPELLE

In that light, it is interesting to consider comments made on the morning of 31 January 1917 by the Germany navy minister Count Eduard von Capelle at a budget committee meeting in the Reichstag. Capelle reminded his colleagues that he had always laid great emphasis on the significance of American entry into the war, but 'from a military point of view her entrance means nothing. I repeat: *from a military point of view America is as nothing*' [emphasis in original].[1] To the hard-liners who pressed for an unlimited submarine campaign, the risk of drawing in the United States was outweighed by the prospect of dealing a decisive knock-out blow to Britain and France before GIs could be deployed 'over there'. Perhaps the remark was tactical, a way of stiffening resolve by playing-down the powers of an opponent, but it may also have been based on incomplete or misleading intelligence. It is also possible that the geographical dispersion of American soldiers throughout the continental states and knowledge of American military deployment in Central America, including a standing force in Nicaragua, where the United States had installed a government, led to a mistaken estimate of actual numbers and battle-readiness. Germany may also have been relying on the sheer width of the Atlantic – America seemed as remote to most Europeans, albeit desirable to some, as Europe now did to the majority of Americans – and on the presence of U-boat squadrons in the Western approaches and in the key sea area around the Azores to prevent a full and successful deployment.

America's first contribution remained her greatest: money. The selling of war bonds yielded sums massive enough to shore up the British at a key moment in the war. But mobilisation moved on apace. By mid-summer more than ten million men had registered for military service of which around one quarter were actually called up in support of the existing services. The exact nature of American involvement had to be settled. As an 'Associated Power' rather than an ally – Wilson was strict and punctilious about this – the US retained a degree of independence from the existing command structure in France. In December 1916, after the disastrous losses at Verdun, General Joseph 'Papa' Joffre had been replaced as commander-in-chief of the French army by General Robert Nivelle, a brilliant artillery officer who had helped prevent a catastrophe in August 1914 and who had come out of the bloody imbroglio of Verdun with some credit. He had devised a plan which he believed would roll back the German salient on the Aisne and allow for quick advances. It involved close co-operation between the British (Nivelle was a Protestant with an English mother) and French, indeed so much so that the British involved in the operation, whose role was to take out German reserves, were effectively fighting under French command. Lloyd George was persuaded; but the British commander Field Marshal Sir Douglas Haig was furious. Like most such dramatic military solutions, the plan worked better in conception than in execution and Nivelle's casual briefing of journalists meant that its details were known to the enemy in advance. Its failure in the late spring of 1917 led to Nivelle's replacement by the charismatic Philippe Pétain, but also left the Allies bloodied and desperate for prompt American help. The eventual aim, as set out by a new Supreme War Council, was to deliver more than a score of American divisions to the Western Front by summer 1918; the shipbuilding programme accelerated by the Navy Act of 1916 meant that their transport and protection *en route* was also more securely guaranteed.

As commander of the American Expeditionary Force (AEF), General John Pershing and his relatively fresh troops had exchanged the hot scrub and the dashing pursuits of the 'Punitive Expedition' in Mexico for the mud and stasis of the Western Front. He arrived to find that Allied commanders expected American troops to be deployed as small self-contained units within existing British and French divisions.

Pershing, who enjoyed considerable freedom of action but in this case reflected his government's strong insistence, made it clear that such an arrangement would not be acceptable and that American troops would, as they arrived, fight as independent commands. The only exception made was for some segregated 'Negro' regiments, which were allowed to fight with the French who already had African troops in the field. Whether Pershing's unwillingness to serve as a supplier of reinforcements made a strategic rather than simply tactical impact is difficult to say. It was clear to the Allies, and particularly to Lloyd George who wrote to Wilson on the subject, that if the Americans were to be effective, their role would need to be co-ordinated with the other friendly powers. A conference was called in Paris for November, and Colonel House was despatched to it as an official representative of the government for the first time.

The Allied situation by now was grave. Pétain had gone some way towards restoring the morale of the French army, but in objective terms the Germans had made advances on the Western Front and the stretching of resources on a line that ran from the Channel Coast almost to the Alps meant that an overwhelming breakthrough – such as that planned by Ludendorff for the spring – couldn't be ruled out. Italy had crumbled and the Bolshevik take-over in Russia presented a new spectre that would require some measure of Allied resistance. There had been some hope that the Kerensky government would continue to prosecute the war in the name of democracy, and indeed the new regime had made promisingly liberal noises about a post-war settlement, arguing against punitive treaties, calls for reparations and wholesale territorial dismantlements. The incoming Bolsheviks were not so even-handedly reasonable; they published full details of pre-war treaties and alliances to demonstrate just how illiberal and grasping the Allied war aims actually were. Having disdained to fight on the same side as a despotic emperor, Wilson now found himself publicly aligned with an imperialistic France and United Kingdom. (He would recall that dilemma when joining the Allies on an anti-Bolshevik – and easily spun as pro-Tsarist – expedition to Northern Russia and to rescue Czech troops stranded in Siberia, even if the latter episode had some spirit-of-1776 gloss to it. Both these engagements continued long after the war in Europe was over and established a pattern of anti-Communist suspicion and hasty policing that some observers see as the start of the Cold War.) That Germany was of a similarly autocratic stamp to the UK and Russia, no one ever doubted – King-Emperor, Tsar and Kaiser were all kinsmen, after all – and in March 1918 Russia found herself bowing to a savage Teutonic imperialism in the devastating Treaty of Brest-Litovsk, a document that would haunt the Paris peacemakers forever, who failed to do much more than echo its moral and political failings.

THE TREATY OF BREST-LITOVSK
The Treaty of Brest-Litovsk was signed between the Central Powers (Germany, Austria-Hungary, Bulgaria and the Ottoman Empire) and Bolshevik Russia on 3 March 1918. Facing collapse at home, the Bolshevik government accepted the most draconian terms in order to end the war. German influence was extended over Poland, Finland, Latvia, Lithuania, Estonia, Belorussia and the Ukraine, depriving Russia of 30 per cent of its pre-war population. Acquisition of territory on such a scale forced Germany to maintain large occupying forces in the East (around one million men), so the Treaty did not free up troops for the Western Front to the extent often believed. The Treaty was formally annulled as part of the Armistice on 11 November 1918.

Once established in Paris, House seemed to feel, with some slight justice, that he had more immediate insight into the smaller and larger barometric changes that rippled through the War Council than did his president in Washington. However, he was also well aware that Wilson would not be budged on either American independence within the 'association' of powers nor on a desire to conduct war and peace on his own terms. Inevitably, those terms had changed since the declaration. Once committed to the war, Wilson had to commit to it wholeheartedly. His difficulty was in balancing an appropriate level of bellicosity – put startlingly in a Baltimore speech given on the first anniversary of the declaration of war as *Force without stint or limit* – with the principle of *peace without victory* and a self-chosen role as peacemaker.[2] Having declined to declare war on Austria-Hungary, and stating openly that the US had no interest in the dissolution of that empire, Wilson now had to ask Congress to authorisation such a declaration, in part to support stricken Italy, in part because the logic of involvement was, as Americans were to discover throughout the remainder of the 20th century, almost always a process of geographical accretion, dangerously unself-contained.

Winning the war was now an urgent imperative, but so too was making some provision for the peace, and Wilson feared any move that would take this out of his control. In the autumn of 1917 Pope Gregory XV had issued a call for peace, disarmament, international arbitration, and a return to the 1914 political map as a means of preserving European civilisation. It is a measure of how far Wilson had travelled, and to what degree his and House's positions had reversed in less than a year that he was unable to subscribe to the Pontiff's plea with any enthusiasm and certainly not to any suggestion that pre-war boundaries could realistically be left unaltered or that the German imperial throne could be left standing; this last issue caused some inevitable unease in London, where any hint of anti-royalism in statement of war aims could be seen to rebound hard on another of Victoria's reigning family. There was a double measure of politics in Wilson's polite but blunt reply to the Vatican. There was a certain suspicion – confirmed in subsequent years – that papal interests leaned to the Central Powers. On the domestic front, Wilson was aware that any call from the Pope would automatically mobilise Irish-American feeling, which was at this juncture still largely anti-British feeling, a problematic situation even for a president not looking to re-election in 1920. Finally and more personally, Wilson regarded himself as an instrument of providence with no less divine warrant than the Bishop of Rome's. He quite simply did not want to see the peace process taken away from him. Nor did he want to see the sometimes contradictory demands of waging war and peace, of political and military independence and 'association', of nationalism and internationalism slip out of proportion one with the other. Making the world safe for democracy remained the aim and required careful pragmatic fixes as well as sounding speeches.

Ironically, the vast proliferation in government business entailed by pre-war diplomacy, then by actual prosecution of the war and domestic support for it led to a shift in Wilson's personal style. In contrast to the imperious self-reliance he had often shown in office, Wilson deferred to a great extent to his war cabinet, relying heavily on the loyal McAdoo, Daniels and Baker on the military side, and the financier Bernard Baruch, who co-ordinated the War Industries Board with great skill. At one level, Wilson – still a notoriously slow reader and absorber of information, and a man whose physical health required frequent breaks and relaxation – simply could not keep pace with the workload. At another level, he could afford to seem somewhat detached from the day-to-day running of the war because his eyes were firmly set on what would happen when it ended. Wilson's portfolio was the future itself.

If he conducted his cabinet meetings, as some colleagues noted, as if he were still at Princeton, still chairing an academic committee or senior common room, Wilson did also appoint a seminar to study the basic principles that would need to be addressed by a peace conference. Shortly after he made his reply to the Pope, Wilson established what became known as 'the Inquiry', an intellectually high-powered think-tank of approximately 150 academics and public intellectuals, the best known of whom now was the youthful *New Republic* editor Walter Lippmann but which also included the historian James Shotwell, the geographer Isaiah Bowman and David Hunter Miller, who advised on legal questions. The group was supervised by House and directed by his brother-in-law Sidney Edward Mezes. A philosopher of Spanish and Italian extraction, Mezes had been president of City College in New York since 1914 and would be part of the American peace mission to Paris. He was also co-author of an 1897 book called *The Conception of God: A Philosophical Discussion of the Nature of the Divine Idea as a Demonstrable Reality,* a title which presumably would have appealed more to Wilson than the later, bluntly titled *What Really Happened In Paris*, to which House also contributed.

House was active in Paris long before any other members of the American delegation. He had tried to prevent Wilson from making further sweeping statements on foreign policy until he returned, but in the meantime 'the Inquiry' was doing its job and on House's return to Washington he found that the committee had made some strikingly un-American suggestions about the future disposition of European territories. This was not the kind of thing the republic was wont to do, but Lippmann, as main drafter of a memorandum to Wilson, had used notably blunt and pragmatic language, advocating the cession of Alsace-Lorraine to France (even if only by way of consolation), the break-up along clearly national lines of the old Austria-Hungary, other less controversial geographical dispositions to Belgium and neutral Denmark, the uncompromising arrest of aristocratic militarism in Germany herself, and, above all, the creation of a great League of Nations first of all to guarantee the protection of European powers from any future revival of that warlike culture but with a place for Germany subsequently should she demonstrate permanently mended ways.

Woodrow Wilson took his copy and with a college professor's instinct for concise exegesis, and in the slightly cumbersome shorthand he had learned to overcome his dyslexia, the president broke down the paper's recommendations into its salient points. There were 14 of them.

ooooo

Always a master of the *bon mot,* Georges Clemenceau – who was later to describe himself as sitting at the Peace Conference between Napoleon (Lloyd George) and Jesus Christ (Wilson) – snorted at Wilson's most famous document. God had given mankind ten commandments and we had failed to keep one of them. How would we fare with Fourteen Points?[3]

There is a tendency to regard them as having arrived to Wilson, entire and graven and direct from God. The first surprise, certainly to anyone who remembered Wilson as a peaceable liberal professor, or even as a neutral president

PRESIDENT WILSON'S FOURTEEN POINTS, 8 JANUARY 1918

The program of the world's peace, therefore, is our program; and that program, the only possible program, as we see it, is this:

I. Open covenants of peace, openly arrived at, after which there shall be no private international understandings of any kind but diplomacy shall proceed always frankly and in the public view.

II. Absolute freedom of navigation upon the seas, outside territorial waters, alike in peace and in war, except as the seas may be closed in whole or in part by international action for the enforcement of international covenants.

III. The removal, so far as possible, of all economic barriers and the establishment of an equality of trade conditions among all the nations consenting to the peace and associating themselves for its maintenance.

IV. Adequate guarantees given and taken that national armaments will be reduced to the lowest point consistent with domestic safety.

V. A free, open-minded, and absolutely impartial adjustment of all colonial claims, based upon a strict observance of the principle that in determining all such questions of sovereignty the interests of the populations concerned must have equal weight with the equitable claims of the government whose title is to be determined.

VI. The evacuation of all Russian territory and such a settlement of all questions affecting Russia as will secure the best and freest cooperation of the other nations of the world in obtaining for her an unhampered and unembarrassed opportunity for the independent determination of her own political development and national policy and assure her of a sincere welcome into the society of free nations under institutions of her own choosing; and, more than a welcome, assistance also of every kind that she may need and may herself desire. The treatment accorded Russia by her sister nations in the months to come will be the acid test of their good will, of their comprehension of her needs as distinguished from their own interests, and of their intelligent and unselfish sympathy.

VII. Belgium, the whole world will agree, must be evacuated and restored, without any attempt to limit the sovereignty which she enjoys in common with all other free nations. No other single act will serve as this will serve to restore confidence among the nations in the laws which they have themselves set and determined for the government of their relations with one another. Without this healing act the whole structure and validity of international law is forever impaired.

VIII. All French territory should be freed and the invaded portions restored, and the wrong done to France by Prussia in 1871 in the matter of Alsace-Lorraine, which has unsettled the peace of the world for nearly fifty years, should be righted, in order that peace may once more be made secure in the interest of all.

IX. A readjustment of the frontiers of Italy should be effected along clearly recognizable lines of nationality.

X. The peoples of Austria-Hungary, whose place among the nations we wish to see safeguarded and assured, should be accorded the freest opportunity to autonomous development.

XI. Rumania, Serbia, and Montenegro should be evacuated; occupied territories restored; Serbia accorded free and secure access to the sea; and the relations of the several Balkan states to one another determined by friendly counsel along historically established lines of allegiance and nationality; and international guarantees of the political and economic independence and territorial integrity of the several Balkan states should be entered into.

XII. The Turkish portion of the present Ottoman Empire should be assured a secure sovereignty, but the other nationalities which are now under Turkish rule should be assured an undoubted security of life and an absolutely unmolested opportunity of autonomous development, and the Dardanelles should be permanently opened as a free passage to the ships and commerce of all nations under international guarantees.

XIII. An independent Polish state should be erected which should include the territories inhabited by indisputably Polish populations, which should be assured a free and secure access to the sea, and whose political and economic independence and territorial integrity should be guaranteed by international covenant.

XIV. A general association of nations must be formed under specific covenants for the purpose of affording mutual guarantees of political independence and territorial integrity to great and small states alike.

is the Points were, indeed, cast as Mosaic commandments rather than as Beatitudes. The pre-war president who refused to premise Europe's and the world's future on 'victory' and who had all but promised that there would be no annexations and no economic penalties was now speaking much more like a victorious punisher.

The Fourteen Points, in fact, represent Wilson less as the agent of providence or as an original thinker, but in his most effective role as a shaper and proponent of ideas already around in the ether and in the culture. The difficulty he had in this case was that too many cultures would be involved at an eventual peace conference, each of them with specific grievances, most of them still hoping for delivery on promises made in the secret diplomacy which Wilson – his very first Point – regarded as first cause of the present conflict. His concern in writing out his commandments was not so much their future breach as their immediate acceptability.

The original memorandum, signed by Mezes, Miller and Lippmann was headed 'The Present Situation: The War Aims and Peace Terms It Suggests'. As the title suggests, the focus was actual and empirical rather than hortatory, and the emphasis very much on how the specific disposition of the combatants at the end of 1917, beginning of 1918 determined the peace terms that might be advanced. For Wilson, pre-war promises were off the table because they had been made under the table, but only in those cases where the victorious power did not have the means to insist. Italy, for instance, was to be denied much of what she wanted from the war, for the devastatingly simple reason that Italy lost. Pacifying France and Britain would not be so easy, and so Wilson and House, the former driven by a need to express a whole liberal worldview in tough and practical terms, as a mediator who was also a belligerent, the latter convinced that he had more immediate insight into the thinking of the various parties, made revisions to the document.

The situation that presented itself at the beginning of 1918 was a highly complex one. Russia had fallen, not just to Germany but to Communism and Wilson had to send out some message to both peoples, assuring the Germans that America did not pursue their destruction and humiliation and also the Russians that America would always support self-determination and freedom from ideological tyranny; he had thought he was doing that in welcoming the Kerensky government, but increasingly the message had more than subtly shifted, now that Germany itself, albeit savagely occupying parts of Russian territory in a non-negotiated peace, was quickly becoming recast as a bulwark against the Red tide. It is as interesting to speculate how a Fourteen Points might have read before the Bolshevik Revolution as it is to consider how they might have been scaled down if drafted at the height of Ludendorff's almost successful spring offensive.

What prevented that succeeding was, in large part British and French doggedness, but also in some significant part the arrival of American troops and the promise of more. The urgency of the war effort, along with the intense ideological effort that accompanied it, was making an even more profound impact domestically. The world's most powerful economy was skewed out of shape. The heaviest demand on fuel coincided with the coldest winter on record. Manufacturing priorities had changed. Commercial transport needs were subordinated to military. Mob violence eventually prompted a 'Statement to the American People' in July 1918, which Wilson's enemies thought was hopelessly overdue. In an anticipation of Republican gains in the November congressional election, the bi-partisanship usually practised in democracies during wartime steadily dissolved, with the powerful figure of Theodore Roosevelt still leading the pack against what was presented as a bungling administration. It was, in fact, a highly effective administration working in *terra incognita* and Wilson's harmonising of interests and of apparently contradictory imperatives – best summed as waging war to secure peace – was virtuosic.

Engineering a consensus had always been Wilson's great goal in politics, though he did not need the consensus of more than a few intimates to convince himself of an idea's worth and viability. Robert Lansing was allowed to make a few changes to the text of the Fourteen Points speech, but for the most part Wilson worked with House on the draft. To what extent the Colonel offered specific suggestions and to what extent he acted mainly as sounding board and foil to Wilson is difficult to judge, given House's own self-aggrandizing account and Wilson's own later negativity, but the joint aim was clear: a speech that would in some way reassure and stiffen listeners not just in Congress, not just in Allied councils, but right across the world to where Trotsky and others were involved in a weird inversion of Wilson's 'peace without victory' concept. As House noted in his diary, the chief concern was to satisfy Britain that her empire was not to be compromised in any way. In the not-so-deep structure of the eventual text, the use of 'must' expressed some assumption of general agreement on a principle or provision, while 'should' flagged a more contentious issue.

Wilson was conscious both of certain opposition at home – Roosevelt and Henry Cabot Lodge both pressed for Germany's unconditional surrender and a dictated peace, while Roosevelt accused Wilson of trading-in patriotism for a vapid internationalism – but also of a dramatically changed situation abroad. Internationalism was already associated in many minds with Bolshevism and Wilson was quickly aware that Bolshevik Russia rather than the crumbling Empire in Vienna now represented a threat to the self-determination of the Czech and South Slav peoples. His own internationalism and instinctive resistance to dramatic change in the *status quo ante bellum* were now confronted not just by the expert opinion of 'the Inquiry', but also by the objective situation, which was highly volatile and in significant respects unprecedented.

The effect of all this, unexpectedly only with the kind of hindsight that sees Wilson as the architect of the League of Nations, albeit an architect who was prevented from seeing it soundly constructed, is that it pushed the League, which it will be remembered was originally proposed by Sir Edward Grey, into the forefront of Wilson's model for peace. Quite simply, the best way to reconcile his conflicted attitude to national and international concerns was to combine the two. By making the League not just a component of the peace but its overdetermining principle, Wilson could temporise with other, more specific proposals. As ever, he was playing politics, and playing shrewdly.

As House had encouragingly predicted, the 8 January 1918 speech to both houses of Congress was mostly well received, and reinforced Wilson's claims to be chief peacemaker when the war ended. Politics is more Babel than Pentecost, however, and Wilson's words were understood and appreciated only inconsistently. The Italian government was predictably unimpressed, believing that Wilson's ninth Point, about the reorganisation of Italy along lines of recognisable nationality, violated promises made at the secret(!) Treaty of London in 1915, which had brought Italy into the war alongside the

Allies. The British were troubled by any insistence on the freedom of the seas and interference in colonial matters. In France, *revanchisme* was on the rise, a mood echoed in the more bullish rows of the Republican benches at home where Wilson's studied reasonableness was seen as an act of surrender rather than a call for surrender. The Fourteen Points arguably made the greatest and most positive impact in Germany, where ultimately they would be accepted as a basis for armistice. The CPI and the military co-operated to drop thousands of the copies of the translated speech behind enemy lines, where it was read with interest and some popular enthusiasm. The German people could expect no quarter from France or Britain, no help from Vienna, and only a looming threat from Moscow, but might reasonably believe that America, set to deliver the fatal blow, but still effectively in mid-Atlantic passage, also offered a way out of complete catastrophe and humiliation. Wilson continued to modulate his rhetoric with a German audience in mind. The Baltimore speech in April was forceful, but, like Jehovah, Wilson implied that the just would be spared from destruction. In September, clarifying his fundamental principles to Congress, he made the politic distinction between the German people on the one hand, the Hohenzollern dynasty and the High Command on the other completely explicit by suggesting that the people's only course was to overthrow their government and bring the war to an end.

According to Sir William Wiseman, a young English baronet and intelligence officer who acted as liaison with the Americans during the war and at the Peace Conference, Wilson had been more squeamish about such an approach in the case of Austria-Hungary, suggesting that America was not good at setting peoples against their leaders, and generally made a 'mess' of it.[4] Some – and Lansing was among them – argued that Wilson made a mess of defining one of his key terms, allowing 'self-determination' to float between half a dozen different interpretations premised on race, territory, ethnicity, language, custom and habit, its undoubted rhetorical force inconsistently attached to known situations. However, under Lansing's influence, Wilson had become increasingly committed to the independence, not merely autonomy, of the Czechs and South Slavs and was working covertly to that end, which the Americans hoped might drive a wedge between Austria and German, breaking the axis and isolating Germany further. Wilson also recognised that given the need for a strong independent Poland as a *cordon sanitaire* between Europe and Communist Russia – how quickly the logic of the 'Cold War' began to function! – it would be inconsistent not to apply the same logic to Czechoslovakia, Hungary and the Yugoslav peoples. Clemenceau rather spoiled things by releasing a letter in which the Austrian emperor seemed to endorse French claims to Alsace-Lorraine. This made further covert negotiation more difficult and the prospect of an early armistice more remote. On the other hand, the military and political situation in the crumbling empire was an objective mess, to which Wilson's approach, typically broad-brush and ruling out the Austrian offer of conditional cease-fires and negotiations, offered no reliable solution. For the moment, in any case, the critical action was elsewhere.

After the bloody failure of the Nivelle offensive in 1917, the Western Front had settled back into stalemate. Germany increasingly leaned toward a policy of what became known as 'strategic defence', no longer looking to make territorial advances, but bunkered in the relatively sophisticated trench and communication system known as the 'Hindenburg Line', there to wear out further the depleted Allied armies. Attrition as fact had turned into attrition as strategy. Only the arrival of American troops seemed likely to break the deadlock. By the early summer of 1918, with British naval help, almost 1,000,000 American soldiers were deployed in Europe.

At Château-Thierry we saved the world.[5] Wilson's claim was of a sort that could only hope to infuriate the Allies, who had been labouring and dying for three years on the Western Front, while the Americans had only just arrived. There is some justice in it, though. The United States' main military involvement in the First World War came as part of what is known as the Second Battle of the Marne in July 1918, the result of a swift German thrust towards Paris. Conscious that time was running out, and persuaded that an attack on men without battle experience might lead to a breakthrough, the Germans launched an offensive against the American sector. Three days later, the AEF under Pershing (though notionally under the overall command of the recently appointed Supreme Commander Marshal Ferdinand Foch) launched a counter-offensive carefully co-ordinated with French and French colonial troops. Its success depended on utmost secrecy in the planning and on the abandonment of the usual initial artillery barrage, which served little purpose on the Western Front other than to warn the enemy of and imminent infantry advance. At Château-Thierry, the Americans left their trenches under cover of a brilliantly executed creeping barrage and moved forward under its protection. So successful was the manoeuvre that the AEF was able to join up with French infantry fighting on a far flank and to push the assault well into enemy-held territory, a rate of progress almost unheard of since the first months of the war and the first of any substance for over a year.

Château-Thierry and Belleau Wood were the US's two main battle honours from the Great War. The fighting in the Aisne-Marne region and round Soissons was both typical and atypical, but either way had little of the qualities of Armageddon, but it underlined that America came to the war with sword as well as shield. A fortnight before the counter-offensive, on 4 July, Wilson had repeated his insistence that America fought with principled disinterest, or rather in the collective interest of mankind, without hope of revenge, tribute or any territorial advantage, but fought with absolute determination against every kind of 'arbitrary' power. That increasingly meant the Kaiser and his high command.

The war has lasted more than four years and the whole world has been drawn into it. The common will of mankind has been substituted for the particular purposes of individual states. Individual statesmen may have started the conflict, but neither they nor their opponents can stop it as they please. It has become a people's war, and peoples of all sorts and race, of every degree of power and variety of fortune, are involved in its sweeping processes of change and settlement. We came into it when its character had become fully defined and it was plain that no nation could stand apart or be indifferent to its outcome. Its challenge drove to the heart of everything we cared for and lived for. The voice of the war and become clear and gripped our hearts.

Woodrow Wilson, Address in New York, 27 September 1918.[6]

There is extensive study of how wars end. The key factors may include simple exhaustion, the actual or imminent destruction of one combatant by another, the intervention of another power or net change in political circumstance. The end of the First World War combined all these factors – with the emergence of Soviet Russia as the radically new geopolitical element – but it was also based on a calculation and compromise. Wilson reiterated his commitment to an impartial and just peace under the guarantee of a League of Nations in a speech made in late September. Ten days later, the Germans responded with a request for peace based on Wilson's various statements and on the Fourteen Points. Wilson drafted a reply that accepted the German note on condition of an immediate withdrawal from all occupied territory. In this, he acted unilaterally, against all advice and without consulting the Allies (but bullying them with the threat that America had the resources to guarantee 'freedom of the seas' by building a fleet even larger than the Royal Navy, and scaring them with the cloudy concept of 'self-determination', which seemed, though even Wilson was inconsistent on the point and hedged it with the qualification 'well-defined', to offer *carte blanche* to nationalist movements everywhere, including the British Empire; in his book on the peace negotiations, Lansing described the coinage as a 'disaster' and claimed, with some prescience, that it would cost thousands of lives).[7] The domestic context to all this was significant. Wilson might be at the apex of his second and final term as president and about to embark on a career-defining mission; the Democratic party was facing crucial congressional elections, and Wilson seemed to be going against a tide of public opinion, stoked by his own propaganda machine, that wanted the war prosecuted with maximum determination. Roosevelt and Lodge now seemed to speak more for the majority than Wilson, and so it proved on 5 November, one month after the German note, when the Republicans regained control of both houses of Congress. Wilson had asked for a vote of confidence (an exceptionally risky tack he had been advised against) and had not received it.

At home, Wilson was a minority president with two hostile chambers ranged against him. Abroad, he was a charismatic peacemaker. In practice, much as he had changed tack on the war once embarked upon it, so too his approach to the peace was more aggressive than he had originally promised, closer in many respects to the punitive settlement demanded by his political opponents, but the paradox of morality and popularity abroad, pragmatism and obloquy at home is one that that has become characteristic of contemporary Western politics. For Wilson it must have seemed giddyingly new and it explains his willingness to leave American shores for six months, delegating domestic affairs to others as he had largely delegated the prosecution of the war, in order to devote himself to a single big idea that set fair to reverse a main tide of American politics since the time of George Washington.

The end, when it came, was a surprise. The Allies and America had counted on fighting on for a time, deploying more of the four million Americans who had been called up, running out the new naval ships and developing a new Wild West in aerial combat over the fields of France, perhaps rolling back the line into German territory before there was any surrender. The breakthrough of 4 August proved decisive and irreversible. After the destruction of 15 infantry divisions during August, the High Command started to look for a way out. After further delay and obduracy, though without much realistic hope of resisting the freshly reinforced Allies (Hitler's 'stab in the back' was more paranoid than real) the Germans took Wilson's cue and forced the Kaiser to abdicate on 9 November. Two days later the armistice was declared on a broad understanding of the Fourteen Points; a broad understanding, that, is, between Germany and the US, not between Germany and the Allies, who still could not accept the Points without amendment. After a further round of discussions, House acceded to key British and French demands, accepting that freedom of the seas be at least discussed at a subsequent peace conference, like that Germany might be

(Right to left) Woodrow Wilson, Georges Clemenceau and Lloyd George on their way to the signing of the Treaty of Versailles, June 1919.

II

The Paris Peace Conference

5

America saved the world …

'Almost everybody in the neighbourhood had "troubles", frankly localized and specified: but only the chosen had "complications". To have them was in itself a distinction, though it was also in most cases a death-warrant. People struggled on for years with "troubles", but they almost always succumbed to "complications".[1]

Woodrow Wilson came to Europe expecting to encounter 'troubles', locally specific needs and demands that would either pass the test of American liberalism and fit the mesh of the Fourteen Points, or they would not. The League of Nations would exist to resolve 'troubles'. Once secret diplomacy was done away with, disarmament generally accepted, fair trade established via the freedom of the seas, 'complications' would simply melt away like a night fog. Such was Wilson's confidence, but unfortunately another of his cardinal principles, that of 'self-determination', meant that the fog simply rolled back in again. The Peace Conference put 'complications' back in the saddle for the remainder of the 20th century and 'complications' signed the death-warrant of Wilson's precious League of Nations.

The President's arrival in France was a perfect Jamesian moment. Henry James himself had said he would happily return to America to die, but that living there was inconceivable, and he died in England instead in 1916, hated by Theodore Roosevelt for sniping at his homeland from a distance.[2] James's friend Edith Wharton, who wrote the words above, survived the war, albeit with *A Son at the Front*. Between them, they had done much to dramatise the often comic, sometimes tragic incomprehension that hung like a veil, or another mist, between Old World and New.

Wilson may well have donned the mantle of Jesus Christ, but he came to Europe as a money-lender. Never has a banker been more rapturously received by those whose IOUs he holds. For a period in 1918 and 1919, he enjoyed a peculiarly modern kind of celebrity, his still-handsome image known and almost worshipped (H G Wells likened him to a Messiah), his words quoted around the globe. Even those who lived in ignorance of him would in all probability find their lives affected by what was decided in Paris. As Wilson toured Europe prior to the conference, he drew vast crowds. Ordinary Frenchmen and -women paid 300 francs for a curbside place to see 'Veelson le Juste' pass by. Even the Italians, who had been less than lukewarm about their allotment in the Fourteen Points, came out as only Italians can. The French who came to greet him off the *George Washington* at Brest prepared a welcome of Napoleonic splendour, but at the end of his voyage, which had been taken up with intense discussion with his Inquiry, there seemed to be a stone in Wilson's heart. His health was uncertain and the task ahead of him seemed terrifyingly immense. It is as if breathing the sulphurous air of post-war Europe suddenly put him in mind of tragedy.

In the Jamesian tragicomedy, Wilson was a classic

Napoleonic Wars, which had done so much to institutionalise the 'secret diplomacy' Wilson saw as the root of future conflict – but it was still a remarkable step for an American president to commit himself to prolonged absence and to trade in America's enormous moral and financial authority – military, too, if it came to that – for a single vote at the conference. This was how Lansing and others saw it, arguing that the United States could wield a greater and more beneficial influence – and maintain her traditional policy of disentanglement – at a distance, advising, admonishing, steering, mediating, but not actually sitting down at cards. Wilson would have none of that. Having committed his second term to this, he would not be absent and he argued that as head of the government, as well as head of state, he had every bit as much right and reason to be there as Clemenceau and Lloyd George. His determination probably weakened his and House's wish that the conference be held on neutral soil, a view he half-shared with the British prime minister who probably wanted the discussions held in London but certainly did *not* want them held in France; on this, though, Clemenceau would not budge.

That Wilson would go to Paris was never in doubt. Who would go with him was more of a question and a matter of some political delicacy. Given that America had voted resoundingly Republican in the congressional elections, it might have seemed appropriate to invite a senior Republican to join the American Commission to Negotiate Peace. Among the more obvious candidates were two former presidents, Roosevelt and Taft; among the other heavyweight contenders were a former secretary of state Elihu Root and the powerful Henry Cabot Lodge, who would later, and with some satisfaction, deal the death blow to American ratification of treaty and League. Though Wilson doubtless understood the value of having the Republicans on board, something that was being pressed on him by both Tumulty and House, he was also aware that Roosevelt wanted Germany humbled, Taft distrusted the Fourteen Points and disagreed with many of their specifics, and Lodge was implacably opposed to the League, to which Wilson now firmly subordinated almost any other consideration, including the peace itself. Root remained an obvious and viable choice, but Wilson chose Henry White instead.

A now somewhat overlooked figure, the Southerner was one of the most gifted diplomats of his generation. Much admired by Roosevelt, who appointed White ambassador to Italy and as chief American mediator at the Algeciras conference, he recommended himself to Wilson because of his neutralist instincts and basic agreement with the principles of the Fourteen Points. Educated in Paris, and with distinguished service at the embassy in London, White and his wife had been in Germany when the war began and were sequestered there for some time thereafter. White had been in semi-retirement after the end of Roosevelt's administration, though he accompanied the former president on an important European tour, which refreshed and consolidated White's contacts there. Wilson tried to tempt him back into diplomatic life as a delegate to the Pan-American Conference in 1914 and as ambassador to Haiti, but White's wife was dying of a neurological disorder and he declined. Wilson was further impressed by White's acceptance of the need for a robust response to the submarine campaign and, once entered on the war, to prosecute it with commitment. In reality, Wilson rarely consulted him in Paris, but as will be seen that was in keeping with his treatment of other, ostensibly closer aides. The President thought highly enough of White to leave him behind in France to continue peace negotiations with Austria-Hungary and Bulgaria, which White did very effectively.

It had been understood that the respective delegations would consist of the head of state or prime minister and either foreign minister or secretary of state. Robert Lansing was the *de facto* head of the American mission, but Wilson would cheerfully have left him behind. He had grown tired of what he considered Lansing's pettifogging obsession with detail and largely excluded him from the more important discussions and decisions. Lansing was an intelligent man and a gifted international lawyer, who had negotiated important agreements regarding Alaska and the Bering Sea, and Japan (the Lansing-Ishii note of 1917 which reaffirmed the Open Door policy in China), and who initiated surveillance (and subsequently) protection of foreign diplomats during the war years, further token of the appetite for clandestinity that had so appalled Bryan. His fundamental difference with Wilson was not so much temperamental and intellectual – though the president's apparent indifference to fact was a barrier to communication and co-operation – but over the League of Nations. Lansing was known to be sceptical, which infuriated Wilson, but more closely examined, it was a thoroughly consistent and logical position: if, as Lansing would argue, there were an equitable and mutually agreed system of international law, there would be no need for a supervening body like the League; Wilson's own grasp of 'jurisprudence' was of a thoroughly Anglo-American sort that required little in the way of supra-national accommodations.

There was, as some commentators have pointed out, a further political dimension to Wilson's refusal to appoint Republicans to the Commission. He intended to conduct negotiations entirely according to his own principles and convictions. If he had, hypothetically, appointed Roosevelt (the old lion actually died in January 1919, as the conference began) or Taft, then any instance of unilateral behaviour would have been taken as a seriously partisan slight. Lansing was a Democratic appointee who could be ignored as required and without significant repercussions, other than a seething resentment. Lansing got his own back after Wilson's stroke in 1919, taking on *de facto* running of the government by calling and chairing cabinet meetings and even suggesting that Vice-President Thomas R Marshall might assume full executive powers given Wilson's incapacity; Wilson took revenge in turn by asking him to leave.

The only military man among the four plenipotentiaries (House's rank was a purely honorary one) was General Tasker H Bliss, who had overseen American mobilisation and then had been appointed to the Allied Supreme War Council. Though past mandatory retirement age, Wilson had promoted and retained him, liking both his efficiency and his devotion to scholarship. Bliss had formerly taught military science at the Naval War College and was devoted to classical historiography. He settled most comfortably into the luxury of their new quarters on the second floor of the Hôtel Crillon, whose Old World splendour sat strangely with the supposedly democratic spirit of the Americans.

Arguably the most important member of the American commission was already in France, occupying the floor above Bliss, Lansing and White and behaving very much like the *éminence grise* he was considered to be; French furniture and food brought out the Mazarin in Colonel House. His large suite was the scene of many discussions with the President who often walked down from his private residence at the Hôtel Murat (despite the names, these were private houses).

Bliss may have been happy to lie in late and read about the Peloponnesian Wars; Lansing and White felt marginalised. Wilson's reunion with House was initially a warm one, to the dismay of Edith Wilson, who had contracted a sharp dislike for her husband's old friend. New wives sometimes distrust old friendships, but it is clear that Edith, a shrewd woman with a realistic grasp of human nature, recognised how self-serving House's loyalty often was. As to her presence in France, it was a privilege not accorded to any other delegation wives; Lloyd George's mistress Frances Stevenson was another notable exception to the rule on the British side. The French considered Edith plump and almost matronly, not quite *chic*, but they recognised a couple in love and appearances together at the St Cloud racetrack – the Conference was not all work – were effective public relations, though in reality while the Wilsons relaxed, Colonel House carried on negotiations in private.

If Edith was shrewd, House was shrewder, a master psychologist and manipulator whose great skills were effectively camouflaged by intense myopia, intense pallor and physical frailty. Worn out by his efforts in the last weeks of the war, he contracted 'flu just before the Conference began and was lucky to pull through; if it was of the 'Spanish' strain that was still killing thousands across the world at this time, he was possibly lucky since it seemed to prey most hungrily on the young and fit. In January 1919 House, having survived an accident-prone Texan childhood, had just turned 60. Like Wilson, he was a Southerner, educated in the North, though he had to drop out of Cornell University when his father went bankrupt. House's first political successes were in his native state, where he acted as kingmaker to four successive governors, an experience that confirmed his natural position was behind the throne rather than on it. Nevertheless, House obviously fantasised about power. In a fascinating anticipation of Harry Turtledove's counterfactual story of Woodrow Wilson as president of the Confederacy, House published (anonymously) a novel called *Philip Dru: Administrator* in which a Cincinnatus-like figure (with hints of Theodore Roosevelt) leads the Western states to victory over the corrupt and plutocratic East. That was in 1912, a year after House met Wilson, by which time he had been in New York for almost a decade.

House made himself indispensable during Wilson's first presidential campaigns, delivering the nomination at least, and Wilson offered him his pick of cabinet posts. At the end of the war he found himself performing the duties of the one job he could not have been offered (since Bryan had to be Secretary of State) but in his usual semi-official capacity. House liked to be 'useful', but had the habit of allowing pragmatic adjustments to harden instantly into new principles; an unfortunate by-product of his conviction that any 'trouble' could be resolved by discussion and compromise was that he was intellectually indisposed to recognise 'complications'. Wilson grew to despair of House's concessions, particularly after his own brief return to America in February 1919 left House in the Council of Ten. The other Allied leaders recognised his abilities, but suspected they were shallow. House distrusted Lloyd George on sight, though perversely he thought that Clemenceau might be the more tractable of them.

When House and Wilson were reunited on 14 December, a day after the President's landing at Brest, the worry that dominated their conversation was that the Allies had already worked out some kind of peace deal at meetings in London which pre-dated the American arrival and smacked uncomfortably of the secret 1915 Treaty of London which brought Italy into the war. Though he attracted equally enthusiastic crowds when he crossed over to Britain, Wilson was affronted that Lloyd George had not come to him in France, somewhat inconsistently so, unless he had simply forgotten or risen above the pressures of domestic politics. The day House and Wilson met in France, Britain went to the polls in an election significantly complicated by a delicate political balance (hence the coalition outcome) and demographically uncertain given the numbers of returning soldiers (hence 'khaki election') and the fact that women were voting for the first time. When the final result was announced, a fortnight later, 18 different parties and independent interests were represented in the House of Commons, which explains Lloyd George's concern over the election.

After House took ill, Clemenceau visited and tried to reassure the Americans that there were no settled accords on the peace and that the London discussions had simply been a courtesy to Lloyd George, who had election matters to deal with. In reality, Britain and France were at odds over colonial issues, particularly the disposition of the crumbled Ottoman Empire, while Italy – in anticipation of the subsequent walkout – was too obsessed with her own territorial claims to see the larger diplomatic picture. Wilson remained suspicious, though, and was frosty almost to the point of rudeness on his trip to London, his old Anglophilia receding in face of his fear and perhaps envy of British imperial power. He was also very displeased by a suggestion that he should visit the former battlefields, believing that the French thought a brisk *douche* of reality and horrors-of-war might shake the President's high-minded liberalism and make him more sympathetic to France's shaky irredentist aims and demand for reparations.

Clemenceau in particular believed that Wilson had grown up in an atmosphere of peace, plenty and both intellectual and physical security and so failed to understand the French mentality, a belief that overlooked the American's Civil War boyhood where the aftermath of carnage was no less horrific than on the Western Front, if on a smaller scale. France had lost more than a million and a quarter men of the younger generation, which would have a marked impact on the birth-rate for 30 years; her agricultural and industrial infrastructure was heavily degraded; her land and people violated.

Wilson in turn increasingly felt that House had misrepresented the situation, and particularly the mood of the two main Allied leaders. He also found it difficult to accept that while both Clemenceau and Lloyd George apparently endorsed the proposed League of Nations, neither regarded it as he did. Wilson saw the League as the agency of a peace settlement, and thus the first item to be settled at the Conference; Lloyd George and Clemenceau saw it as a subsequent guarantor and thus not an urgent priority. This was compounded by quibbles about how the terms would be discussed before negotiations began with the Germans. It was Wilson's assumption that there would be negotiations with the vanquished power; again the European Allies disagreed, asserting something like the old Congress of Vienna 'balance of power' model (which Clemenceau knew would infuriate Wilson for whom such an arrangement was the *radix malorum*) and continued furthermore to speak of the League in terms that more closely resembled the post-Second World War North Atlantic Treaty Organisation (NATO) than Wilson's global community.

Wilson's brand of charisma was very different to Clemenceau's, and to Lloyd George's. The old French tiger was characterised by his courage and his coal-black hatred of Germany, while Lloyd George seemed to have a touch of necromancy about him, an impression sealed for ever by Keynes's bizarre description of 'this syren, this goat-footed bard, this half-human visitor to our age from the hag-ridden magic and enchanted woods of Celtic antiquity'.[5] Of the three, only Wilson seems unambiguously human, defined and limited by light and reason, perhaps also limited by his very humanity and resistance to ambiguity. From the very beginning, Clemenceau and Lloyd George were repelled by his assumption that peace could be delivered according to what looked like a mathematical formula or a catechism. This is to overlook that all three were pragmatists at bottom, albeit highly self-sufficient pragmatists who took advice only sparingly, with Wilson no less determined and cunning than the others. Mythology, though, is often stronger than political reality.

In London, Wilson had been at pains to underline the old saw about Britain and America being divided by a common language, suggesting that only mutual interest held them loosely together. In Paris, there was a predictable discussion over what language discussions and negotiations should be conducted in, though the outcome was slightly surprising. Wilson (who spoke good French) and Lloyd George (who spoke virtually none) felt that English was becoming an international tongue, supplanting French as the *lingua franca* of international diplomacy. The Italians seemed affronted, which prompted Lloyd George to suggest mischievously that the Japanese – who were also present at the first meetings – would be entitled to feel affronted as well, though they showed no signs of it. Another 30 nations – and probably a dozen language groups – would be represented at the Peace Conference, though not Russia, still at war with herself and the West, and only present in the form of a delegation of exile and minority groups. The seeds of future conflicts were being sown, though, as Lansing had feared: the future Ho Chi Minh was nearby working as a kitchen porter at the Ritz and anxious to test Wilson's principle of self-determination in the case of his native Vietnam. The harmony of nations, already showing discord over matters of precedence – delegate numbers were inconsistently assigned – was threatened with Babel. Russian would not be heard. The end of the Allied war with Germany effectively overturned the Treaty of Brest-Litovsk, but the Bolshevik government would not parlay with Western powers who were still sending troops and support to the White and Tsarist opposition. Russia's absence meant that no Cyrillic copies of texts would be required. It also meant that any treaty was fatally compromised in one vital aspect. Unexpectedly, Clemenceau agreed to English, perhaps because it gave him a chance to show off his fluent and faintly slangy Americanisms; he had married and divorced an American girl, Mary Plummer, who had died in 1917.

The more pressing practical issue was not in what language they would speak, but in what form. Wilson, who saw no actual obstacles to the implementation of the Fourteen Points, was anxious to keep the discussions relatively informal and thus paradoxically closed. His hatred of secrecy did not necessarily extend this far and he was fearful what the American press corps might make of the kind of discussion he had been hearing in the Supreme Council, or Council of Ten.

This consisted of the French, British and Italian prime ministers, the American president, along with their foreign secretaries, as well as representatives of Japan, whose presence had been requested by Britain. The Council met in the Quai

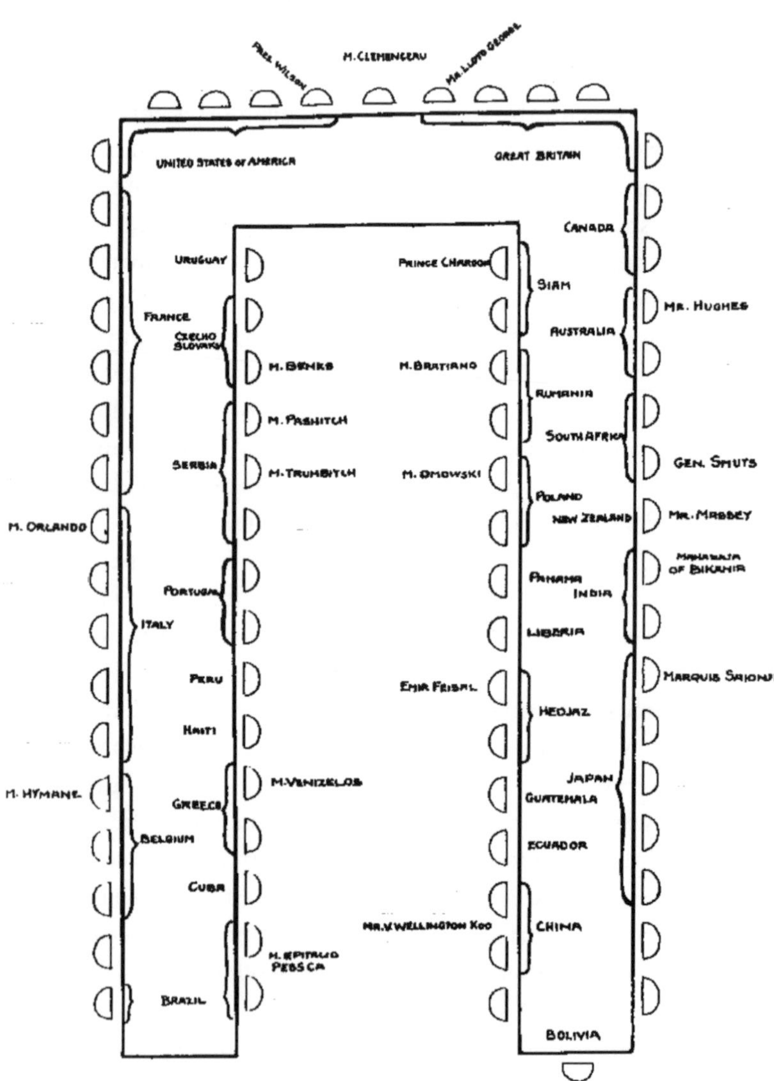

Sketch of the seating plan at the Paris Peace Conference.

d'Orsay offices of Stéphen Pichon, the foreign minister who had met Wilson at Brest and who, somewhat like Wilson with Lansing, Clemenceau affected to forget at every opportunity, preferring the company of his 'House', the real General Henri Mordacq. As a head of state, Wilson sat in a higher chair than the others, but often fidgeted and paced around while Clemenceau, playing on his nearly-80 years, acted the grand old man, fiercely insistent when he had a point to make, affectedly deaf or sleepy when he did not want to hear another's point of view. The absence of Russia, albeit as a catastrophically defeated ally, was an early issue for the group, with Lloyd George suggesting that the Bolsheviks and their opponents be invited to the conference. Wilson supported him, but Clemenceau, Foch and the Italian prime minister Orlando were ferociously opposed. Allied intervention against the Bolsheviks was curiously half-hearted and inconsistent, as Winston Churchill, a member of the British Empire delegation, noted angrily, echoing a sarcastic message to Wilson sent in the last month of the war by the clever Georgi Chicherin, who had replaced Leon Trotsky as Commissar for Foreign Affairs. Though the sixth of the Fourteen Points had called for evacuation of Russian territory (Germany and Japan had both held Russian land) and Wilson had been quoted as saying that Russia's problems were an internal matter that only the Russians could deal with, he had also agreed to send American troops to aid anti-Bolshevik forces and he was committed to non-recognition of the new regime. Arguably, nowhere – apart from Austria-Hungary – better illustrated both the potency and the vacuity of Wilson's faith in 'self-determination'. His compromise suggestion, an abortive one in the event, was that the Russians (including representatives of both the old and new regimes) meet with a delegation from the Council of Ten on the island of Prinkipo, near Istanbul in the Sea of Marmara. 'Self-determination' collided with 'world revolution' just as both were revealed to be unworkable.

There was also the vexed question of Germany's former colonies. Wilson was appalled by any suggestion of annexation, aware that the British Dominions of South Africa and Australia had already cast envious eyes on South-West Africa and on the Bismarck archipelago, Germany's widely scattered Pacific colony; in face of Wilson's opposition, General Jan Smuts had suggested a compromise – actually, a self-serving compromise – whereby certain territories would best be administered under the laws and control of the country holding the mandate, which was annexation by any other name. Wilson's hope was that such territories could become League of Nations mandates, but as with the Russian situation he seems to have let this one drift by him as well. The reason was written large in his approach to the colonial problem. For Wilson, the League and the drafting of its Covenant came before any other issue.

Wilson's ability to deliver such a draft and secure its early passage was one of his few signal triumphs. However, the relative ease with which he got the Covenant past the first plenary session of the Conference on 14 February, immediately before he had to return to the United States to deal with essential constitutional business, was also a measure of the document's fatal emptiness of detail. It was Wilson's belief that the *principle* of the League, premised on the *word* of all the signatories, and backed only very remotely by the sanction of military force, would be enough to guarantee world peace. In truth, there was insufficient substance to the draft Covenant to attract much serious opposition from the Allied leaders, who were more concerned with peace terms than with the idea of the League. In America, the mood was rather different.

ooooo

Winston Churchill had desperately tried to secure some clear answer to the Allied position on Russia, suggesting that shilly-shallying was a disaster and only determined military action served any good. He made his own intervention at the Supreme Council just as Wilson was making what would be his final address before returning to the US. Wilson had his Covenant and his mind was turning to the matter of persuading Congress to accept it as an indissoluble element of the treaty, so he was not much minded to heed a young Englishman of aristocratic background (albeit with American connections) harping on the old song of war.

Wilson left for home later that day. Lloyd George could slip back and forth across the English Channel to deal with domestic affairs, and left for London himself in hopes of averting a general strike. Wilson, though, had a longer voyage and faced a more uncertain reception. He received a decent welcome in Boston – Henry Cabot Lodge's power-base – and gave a ringing speech that invited Americans to take pride in their new-found status as the world's friend and its best hope, but also to take responsibility for the world's future security by backing the still negotiable League Covenant, which he had described in Paris on 14 February as a 'vehicle for life' rather than a 'straitjacket', but in particular its non-negotiable Article X, which called for collective responsibility for world peace and offered a 'definite guarantee' that this could be achieved.[6]

Now, though, as later in the year, he would have to

convince the Congress of these things; without its approval, well-received speeches and public ovations were as nothing. House had recommended that he address senators and representatives informally first, to gauge the mood and exercise persuasion where it was needed. House remained in France and in Wilson's absence turned once again to the Russian question, despatching William C Bullitt and the journalist Lincoln Steffens to Moscow to sound out the new regime. They came back with a deal of sorts – Allied withdrawal in return for Lenin's 'promise' not to interfere with the White governments – and with a famously positive view of the Bolshevik future: 'it works'. The prevailing American view in Paris (Lloyd George seemed to share it) was that Bolshevism was little more than a symptom of malnutrition and could be eliminated with the application of some good American food; well-fed Bolsheviks would turn into Scandinavian-style social democrats overnight. An aid plan, put together by the tireless Hoover and fronted by the charismatic Norwegian explorer Fritjof Nansen was the preferred approach. Though courteous towards Nansen, the Russians basically spat the deal back in the Allies' faces. Bullitt was ignored and took aggrieved revenge later by collaborating with Sigmund Freud on a psychobiography of Wilson; his disillusionment, to be fair, also had much to do with the savage terms imposed on Germany. The Russian question was never settled at Paris and remained open when the Treaty was signed. Many ironies loom out of it: Wilson was wrong about Russia; Bullitt and Steffens were right in their way, and so, perhaps, was Clemenceau, though for a different reason; Lloyd George was fatally complacent; most piquant of all, the Soviet Union did eventually join the League of Nations, while the United States did not.

Wilson knew he would meet with opposition and on his

return to Washington organised a White House dinner for members of the foreign affairs committees in the Senate and House, but here, too, the application of good American food failed to overcome strong conviction. Two days later, on 3 March, Lodge, who four days after Wilson's Boston speech had spoken in the Senate of America's abandonment of George Washington in favour of Leon Trotsky, drew up a 'Round Robin' criticising the Covenant, in particular its implicit limiting of American independence, and quickly gathered the signatures of more than one third of the Senate, enough to prevent the ratification of any measure.[7]

Wilson was damaged at home, but he was also damaged in Paris, where news of the 'Round Robin' raised significant questions about his leadership, not so much of his own country as of the conference. The logic was straightforward: Woodrow Wilson had premised the peace process on the League, against the better judgement of his fellow leaders, but now his own countrymen did not seem to want the League; was the peace hanging on a frayed cord, or was it simply that Wilson himself was marked down for failure? It was to avert immediate failure that, once back in Paris and in the discussions over the Covenant that ran through late March and April, Wilson entered into the kind of negotiation he despised, trying to make a special reservation in the Covenant for the Monroe Doctrine, which as far as the French were concerned was covered by the clause stating that all international agreements should be in accord with League principles. Others rightly suggested that if a reservation were made on behalf of the United States, then should there not be reservations for any power in a similar position. Sir Robert Cecil, the British diplomat in charge of negotiations for the League of Nations, cleverly suggested that the Monroe Doctrine was only mentioned for purposes of illustration. Wilson himself spoke up passionately about America's shining record in the defence of freedom, but he knew that the reservation was there almost solely for the purpose of getting the Covenant past Congress, which he believed to be guaranteed. The League question was a perfect illustration of Wilson's twin vices of going it alone with scant regard for the advice or opinions of others, and a tendency to think in broad generalities, as if he were asking the people simply to ratify an idea and allow him – or some lesser mortals in government – to handle the detail later on. Wilson was very conscious that the idea of a League of Nations was not initially his, but Sir Edward Grey's, and that there were competing models for it, some of them much more practical in tone than his own, most of those in some way reflecting the nationality and national interests of the author. Léon Bourgeois had drafted a proposal which called for a League with its own army, which answered two French needs in one: an appetite for punitive or *revanchiste* actions, and a recognition that two heavy defeats within 40 years had placed France in need of international policing and protection. In the United States, the League to Enforce Peace was a mixture of Wilsonian idealism and old-fashioned Monroe Doctrine independence of action; as such, it had some bipartisan support. In the UK, peace groups were mostly on the liberal left while an official report under Sir Walter Phillimore sketched out a model that had emphatic – indeed, compulsory – powers of arbitration but which was not simply a congress of the victorious Allies set up as a guarantee against renewed German aggression. Wilson dismissed Phillimore's report because it threatened to steal his thunder and was in any case too burdened with detail.

It was much harder to dismiss Jan Smuts' 'A Practical

Suggestion', a brilliantly expressed position paper which posited a new world order premised on the United Kingdom and the United States, with France a notional third wheel. Smuts set out a potential structure for an international peace league, with a definite mechanism for dealing with disputes and two tiers of membership, with an undifferentiated general assembly of all the world's sovereign nations and a very much smaller executive council presumably dominated by the three imperial or neo-imperial powers. As a South African, Smuts was much concerned by the status of the colonies, proposing a system of mandates for those territories not yet prepared for self-government. In addition to German South-West Africa, which he believed should be under Empire control, Smuts had a particular concern with the Middle East, for which Allied plans had been embarrassingly revealed by Trotsky's cheerful lifting of the lid on secret wartime diplomacy. The question of mandates was a troubling one because it in turn lifted the lid on greedy territorial ambitions. The Australian premier Billy Hughes, who Wilson disliked on sight, demanded Germany's Pacific islands as recompense for the ANZAC sacrifice (and, privately, because the Japanese were present, as a bulwark against Japanese imperialism). New Zealand wanted Samoa, and was in fact already there. The French let all this go on, waiting their turn to hand in a list of former German colonies in Africa and of territories in the Middle East where they believed the tricolour should be flying.

Wilson not only could not ignore Smuts' pamphlet. He incorporated much of it into his own proposals for the League. He then pushed his draft through the commission in less than three weeks, a level of haste dictated not just by his need to return to the US but also his insistence that the League reflect a personal vision rather than a loose amalgam of national interests. The commission was set up on 25 January with Wilson in the chair, supported by House, and representatives of the five Council powers plus representatives from five of the smaller powers, including Portugal and Belgium. Clemenceau and Lloyd George saw no need to be present, though the French prime minister, who liked the idea of the League but professed not to believe in it, worked on the assumption that the League's executive council would indeed be a continuation of the wartime alliance; Bourgeois sat in his stead and argued as best he could for a League with both authority and teeth. Though he was determined that his own version of the League should prevail, Wilson had been obliged to acknowledge how much of its armature came from British sources, so he put together David Hunter Miller and the clever ascetic Sir Robert Cecil to agree a draft that would not admit of any division-by-common-language. Cecil was also dealt an ace card to use against the French: if you continue to obstruct or to make unreasonable demands, the post-war settlement will fall *de facto* to a new alliance between the UK and USA. Cecil was not the only observer to find Wilson peremptory and deaf to argument; even House, whose standing with Wilson was less than it had been and would decline further still, remained silent during commission sessions. So did the Japanese. Wilson was endlessly impatient with French attempts to go over points that he had already ruled against – most often the utterly un-American suggestion that the League rather than Congress could order US troops into action – though he did largely agree with the French belief that Germany should not initially be allowed to

'The whole world wants peace. The President wants his League. I think that the world will have to wait.'

ROBERT LANSING

join the League and would only be admitted when she had served some time in the wilderness.

The Covenant was adopted on 28 April. It snowed outside. Whether the superstitious Wilson, who regarded 13 as his lucky number and therefore his arrival in France on 13 December, the finishing on the draft Covenant on 13 February and its 26 (13 x 2) clauses as good omens, was perturbed by this unseasonal phenomenon is not known, though he was not enjoying the cold. Wilson had gained his first and greatest objective and with the riders that he believed would make it acceptable at home. On 20 March 1919, Robert Lansing wrote in his diary 'The whole world wants peace. The President wants his League. I think that the world will have to wait'.[8] Wilson always believed that even a bad peace could be put right by a good League. The world was waiting, and in other rooms, away from the League commission, a 'bad' peace, rife with 'complications' was unfolding.

6

The present tides

The Congress of Vienna in 1815 carried out its business briskly, with naked self-interest and behind closed doors. There was plenty time left over for lavish entertainment, banquets, balls and other gatherings. To that degree, social life for the peacemakers in Paris was not so very different. In 1919, the city lived up to its reputation for pleasure. Or rather, a large press corps, augmented by literary celebrities like the author Elinor Glyn, helped to reinforce the image of a Paris poised between the City of Light and the Cities of the Plain. There was a puritanical streak to the observations of some American journalists, who pointed out that with many millions dead or maimed, millions more dispossessed or displaced, and whole populations on the brink of starvation, there was something distasteful about seeing politicians lecture the world on peace, disarmament and self-determination before going off to the next in an endless round of dinners, teas, dances, and theatre shows. In fact the delegates worked extremely hard, and Wilson for one had to be dragged to social functions by Edith, or forced to rest by Cary Grayson, but others in the American party partook of the available hospitality as much as possible and set aside as much of their democratic plainness as they dared in the circumstances.

As always, the press's biggest issue was access. The Peace Conference was observed and written about like no comparable event in history. The testimony of participants – D H Miller, House, Bullitt, the Englishmen Harold Nicholson and John Maynard Keynes – lent the attempt to bring peace the same iconic and very literary quality that the Western Front had derived from the 'war poets'; Keynes in particular, and Nicholson more circumstantially, did much later to create the received view of the Conference as producing a botched and vindictive half-peace, foredoomed to be broken. With so many other pens around in Paris, Wilson feared for his own literary efforts and his own iconic texts: the Fourteen Points and the League Covenant. When it became clear that Wilson would not give them a story they turned on Wilson himself, or just as often on Mrs Wilson. The President was convinced, and with some justice, that the French government was stirring up negative publicity about him and passing on details about Edith that cast her in a negative light. Her clothes and manners were disapproved of, she exerted too much influence, and she lacked the *esprit* of Lloyd George's daughter Olwen, who came on a visit and charmed the French premier.

Relations between the US and France were worsening and the press was aware that domestically Wilson was in an increasingly insecure position. Though Roosevelt (who had been a near-certain Republican candidate in 1920, despite his age and previous terms) was out of the way, and despite the fact that Wilson had had to rely on the support of Taft, who believed firmly in the League, on his short visit home, his and the Democrats' position was not strong. Clemenceau even gave a briefing to an American journalist complaining of the waste of time. The old tiger believed there was a job to be done. He pointed out, accurately enough that while much – in the case of iron ore, almost all – of the French industrial infrastructure had been destroyed by the war, German territory had never been breached and her industry was largely intact. That meant Germany was an economic winner, whose position was being strengthened by the slowness of the conference.

It was a shrewd move. Other coups were more fortuitous. On 19 February, while Wilson was in America, Clemenceau was shot at and wounded by an anarchist called Eugène Cottin who declared that he wanted to rid the world of a man who wanted to take the world back to war. Clemenceau escaped death very narrowly indeed, took charge of his own recovery (he trained as a doctor, but never practised) and was back at work before Wilson returned, pardoning his attacker and suggesting that if this was the quality of French shooting, one hit out of seven shots, it was no wonder the war had gone on so long. It was not even possible to level the New World's familiar charges of hedonism and idleness at Clemenceau, who survived on porridge and boiled eggs and chaired sessions with vigour and authority.

Though Wilson noted that the old man seemed shaken by the *attentat*, he himself could barely match him for energy and determination. Wilson functioned best when the tide was full behind him. He was not good when it ebbed, and he was not good at explaining himself in the face of hostile criticism. One either understood and accepted the Wilson gospel or one did not. He saw no reason why a single clause of it should be subject to petty forensic quibble. Despising his sickly Secretary of State – Lansing had diabetes – almost as much as he despised the press, Wilson put them together, leaving Lansing to give briefings while House negotiated points of substance. Lansing never forgot or forgave. Wilson was having doubts about House as well and blamed him for the failure of the White House dinner intended to win round opponents of the League; its failure was entirely due to Wilson's preaching style – if Lansing was excessively legalistic, Wilson was ever more clerical and inflexible. Speaking to the Democratic National Committee in Washington, he had referred to opponents of the League as *blind* and *provincial*, *the littlest and most contemptible* of creatures, and in his Boston speech, he had painted a biblically vivid picture of the man who tried to resist *the present tides* (he was speaking of Henry Cabot Lodge) as being cast utterly alone on some high and barren beach, as far from God as he was from any human consolation.[1]

Wilson returned to Paris on 14 March and was driven to his new quarters – Franco-American relations were straining and the Princess Murat had asked for her house back – on the Place des États-Unis. He was grim-faced, not about the change of residence, but because the evening before, House had come over to Brest to greet him off the *George Washington* with the news that he had given away many concessions to the British and French. They were not binding, of course, without the President's approval, but if he were seen to be welching on deals made in apparent good faith by his proxy, his standing would be further diminished. He had left House in charge, now an official delegate, while he was away. Balfour had led the British effort in Lloyd George's absence, and Clemenceau was coming to meet with both men when he was attacked. In the leaders' temporary absence, they had tried to move ahead with conference business trying to draw up terms for Germany (it was still assumed the Germans would be at the negotiating table shortly), working on the text of the Covenant and creating the territorial commissions that would decide how post-war Europe and beyond would look. House allowed himself to be outflanked and they got no further than the outline of a very harsh treaty.

Remarkably, perhaps, though the armistice was still only that, and until February 1919 had to be renewed every month, there was still talk of resuming war against Germany, whose remaining army had retreated in reasonably good order and with its command structure intact and whose people had seen no entirely convincing evidence of defeat, which usually involves occupation of some sort. Pershing, who perhaps felt cheated of a greater triumph, believed the Allies should push on into German territory. The French were anxious that even a blockaded Germany was capable of regrouping and fighting back, particularly now that the Allies were rapidly demobilising. Wilson, Lloyd George and Smuts were all haunted by the spectre of 'Prussian militarism' somehow joining hands with Russian revolutionism, a mood which pointed as much towards fresh war – and it is anachronistic to suggest that the 'unfinished' or continuous war scenario was only recognised in hindsight in 1939 or 1945 – as it did towards a forgiving peace.

Wilson, despite his image as the apostle of peace, was not prepared entirely to forgive. He hated war, but he believed in retribution. The strains that were becoming evident between Wilson and the French were not, as often suggested, fundamental differences on how to deal with Germany. Wilson and his CPI had gone to considerable lengths during the war to portray the Germans as inhuman foes and Wilson had a high and barren beach marked out for them as well. What he did have, that the jaundiced – or simply more experienced

– French did not, was a sense that the League and its embodied principles represented the agency of a working providence that could deliver punishment but with the promise of a forgiving embrace to come. Germany was to take her whipping, as far as Wilson was concerned, and then to found a place in the new community of power. The extent of that power was discussed while he was in America, with the French pushing for the retention of only a small German army of short-term conscripts. The British representative on the committee charged with the question, Henry Wilson, Chief of the Imperial General Staff, argued for a larger volunteer force, arguing that a more rapid turnover merely created a body of men trained in soldiering who might quickly be called up or used in militias. The compromise arrangement of a small conscript force seemed to please no one. Whether individual Germans, from the Kaiser downward, were to be whipped – or hanged – was a question that exercised the Allies for some time. Lloyd George recognised that talk of hanging Wilhelm II made for headlines every bit as good as those about squeezing Germany till the pips squeaked. In his account of the Council of Four (as they became at the end of March), Paul Mantoux quotes Wilson as solemnly reminding Lloyd George, Clemenceau and Orlando that beheading a bad king had simply created the cult of Charles the Martyr. He probably also had little appetite for endless briefings by Lansing on the legal pitfalls of prosecutions for war crimes; in the event, there were few, most of them minor, and the Kaiser lived on to see Hitler, madder even than himself, take bloody revenge on France.

The question of how Germany might be limited geographically as well as militarily was even more controversial. Wilson's principle of self-determination worked as it was intended to in Schleswig-Holstein, a region that seemed to represent in emblematic form the tortured diplomacy of the Old World, where a plebiscite restored the Danish speaking population of Northern Schleswig to neutral Denmark. A similar plebiscite, which led to the annexation of Eupen and Malmédy to Belgium (some feared that the Belgians, who as first victims of the war, felt aggrieved and overlooked, wanted to annex Luxembourg), was marred by intimidation of German-speaking voters. The issues were more contentious when they touched on the French economy and the question of French security. France wanted the Saar region to replace the coal mines that had been destroyed in the war and Clemenceau, contrary to his implacable image, was willing to countenance some level of co-operation between France and a demilitarised Germany to redevelop the devastated regions. Foch, however, was insistent that the Rhine was a natural – and defendable – boundary, one that marked the old division of Germany and Gaul, and that a neutral Rhineland, with its independence guaranteed by the French, British and Americans, was the only way to protect France's esastern border from any resurgence of German militarism. The old anti-clerical in Clemenceau led him to suspect the nature of the (mostly Catholic) separatist movement that argued for an independent Rhineland, but he let his troops deal with them as they might, continuing to argue that France needed to control the all-important river bridgeheads. Wilson regarded much of this as a kind of category-error. Given the existence of the League, such questions were nothing short of semantically empty. The League would guarantee France's border; the League would protect the neutral countries; the League would ensure that Germany would not re-arm and turn aggressive. There was also a practical and moral question: given that Poland would occupy and own the huge Silesian coalfields on Germany's eastern border, how was Germany to survive, and did further annexation not represent unwarrantable punishment of a vanquished people? The President cabled House and told him to make no agreement on the Rhineland until he returned to Paris.

When he did return, he and Lloyd George told Clemenceau that the United States and Britain would come to France's aid if she were attacked by Germany, but that France had to renounce claims on the Rhineland. Clemenceau – who remembered how quickly the Schlieffen Plan had swept German forces across Belgium and into his country – was concerned that such help would come quickly enough. Lloyd George promised a Channel Tunnel. One advantage of being a half-human Celtic spirit visiting the modern world from antiquity was that such magical solutions sounded half-way plausible. The French were not satisfied. Things came to a head on 28 March. Lloyd George had been trying to broker terms which did not lead to the destruction of Germany – Francophobia was as instinctive as belief in the Royal Navy – and Wilson was arguing that annexation of German territory was in breach of the Fourteen Points, on which basis the armistice had been signed. Clemenceau accused the President of pro-German sympathies, which was damaging because it was half-true. Angry words were exchanged. Wilson asked if Clemenceau wanted him to leave. Clemenceau said no, he was leaving instead, and stamped out. He later delivered a mostly gracious apology, but Wilson's resolve and equanimity were wearing down.

If he ever after believed that House had in some way gone behind his back, there was some merit in the suspicion. The Colonel had helped establish a secret committee on the Rhineland question. The British representative came as close as diplomatically possible to saying that French control of the region simply made France too strong, which Britain could not accept. The committee settled nothing, beyond the recognition that here was an issue that would require protracted discussion. House could only pass on to Wilson the suggestion that immediate peace terms be struck with Germany, leaving the question of territory and reparations for later, which Wilson would have recognised meant without American involvement; as the recent trip had underlined, he had to return home permanently sooner rather than later and, again, the League Covenant, still to be passed, would provide for all eventualities in this case. Tumulty had tried to argue that reparations were an entirely European matter and one that the United States could not only afford to leave, but must leave, to the European powers. Wilson had included 'no punitive damages' in his Fourteen Points and was anxious to see that this was observed. Wilson tried to buy time and even threatened to veto the agreement on Germany's volunteer army. Lloyd George countered with a threat to block the League, and Wilson had to cave in.

The Americans were even more sensitive on naval matters. The British were adamant that naval supremacy was not just a necessity to protect the Empire but to guarantee world peace. The Americans, with Josephus Daniels easily able to get shipbuilding programmes – which amounted to job-creation schemes in cities with naval yards, and many other collateral benefits – through Congress, were quite prepared and able to create a fleet that exceeded the Royal Navy, and it was a threat kept in reserve, not least to mask embarrassing issues such as the proposed internationalisation of the Kiel Canal, a measure which would have cast an embarrassing light on American control of the Panama Canal (though that in turn was neatly covered by the all-important Monroe Doctrine reservation). If the arrest and internment of the German fleet at Scapa Flow had a certain air of poignant drama, some naval discussion bordered on the farcical, when it did not seem simply greedy. The dismantling of German submarines was seen as a prize contract, guaranteeing work for several of the Allies, but Wilson, whose country had ostensibly been drawn into the war by the submarine campaign, wanted building of these sinister craft to be halted altogether, an early instance of a now-familiar American belief that the United States could not only arm the world, but also insist on what arms particular nations would be allowed to hold. The question of Dune and Heligoland, two tiny islands in the North Sea which had become strategically important to Germany, raised some very odd suggestions. Some argued for the islands' destruction, perhaps with the kind of massive mine that had been used to blow up German positions on the Western Front. Others argued for simple demilitarisation. Wilson, sucked into the argument willy-nilly, said that it would be a pity if the sea-defences were destroyed along with the fortifications: where would fishermen shelter from storms? Clemenceau, perhaps joking, perhaps trying to annoy Wilson or possibly Lloyd George, suggested they be annexed to Australia, not so very absurd a suggestion given that they had come into German hands in 1890 in exchange for Zanzibar! Sir Edward Grey, a passionate ornithologist, proposed their use as a nature reserve for migratory birds. Such discussions must have been death to the American President's spirit.

Wilson remained a progressive at a time when not just war and revolution, but also an ever-moving economic and cultural cycle had given progressivism a certain tarnish. Events and circumstance seemed ranged against him. It was said that he aged ten years in a day after hearing of House's concessions to the French, but it has to be wondered whether what observers were seeing was the realisation – delayed until quite away from home – that his confidence in the support of the majority of Americans for the League was more hope than actual. House has taken the blame for Wilson's discomfiture and for disloyally going behind his back. The 'break' between them, ostensibly fomented by Edith, was never as absolute as is sometimes suggested. The coolness that fell was more a function of Wilson's growing remoteness from all as he saw his dreams turning to ash. House had been instructed to negotiate on military terms with Germany but not to go further. There had been problems with communication while Wilson was in America, some of his (coded) messages coming through as corrupt text. Also, House was under some pressure not to waste more time. Finally, though this is perhaps a lesser factor, he was persuaded – not without some justice – that his negotiating skills were greater than the President's but was outmanoeuvred by the wily French. Wilson himself would come under the same pressure on his return and would learn that the world no longer spoke – or perhaps Europe never had spoken – the open-hearted language of the American Progressive Era.

Either way, House remained a loyalist and there remained plenty for him to do. However, there was about to be a great change in the way the highest diplomatic discussions were conducted. At the end of March, the Council of Ten gave way to the Council of Four. Clemenceau, Lloyd George and Orlando began to meet (usually twice a day), mostly in Wilson's office, sometimes in Clemenceau's, with just an interpreter, Paul Mantoux, and occasionally a secretary present. The Japanese appear not to have minded. Everyone was glad to be rid of the Italian foreign minister Sidney Sonnino, whose mood was seldom better than black. Wilson always thrived better in small groups and in situations where he could air ideas without prejudice; the atmosphere was closer to that of a Princeton doctoral committee. The other powers grumbled, but accepted. The decision had been taken partly to speed up the process but also to avoid leaks to the press which, since they were nearly always made by some with a grievance, were mostly negative in cast. Wilson, in particular, was coming in for heavy blows in the French press.

The stories turned particularly sarcastic when Wilson ordered the *George Washington* to return to Brest and, through his press secretary and future biographer Ray Stannard Baker, leaked the story that he might abandon the conference and travel home. He had been taken ill on 3 April and its effect was to plunge him into a depression. Recent historians have set considerable store by the impact of this infection, which seems not to have been pandemic 'flu but some other viral pathogen with a lowering effect on the sufferer's spirits. Even more significant was what may have been another minor stroke, which occurred at the height of the squabble over terms to Germany and left Wilson grey, irritable, fussy and ill at ease. Grayson listened to his patient imagining what the world would be like if the French were simply allowed to have their way; the implication was that he no longer cared and might as well leave Europe to its fate. In private, Lloyd George and Clemenceau, even Orlando, whose own grievances were slowly fermenting, were delighted by Wilson's temporary absence; his high-minded stubbornness was becoming tiresome. Clemenceau likened him to the valuable cook who keeps her trunk packed in the hallway, ready to resign at a moment's notice if she is thwarted.[2] The sarcasm hid a recognition: that Wilson was still invaluable to the Conference.

If Clemenceau was delighted to be free of American quibbles and hectoring for a couple of days, his delegation was more concerned about the implications of an American walk-out, or even of Wilson's personal disengagement (both options were possible) and the censors limited comment in the papers. The virus Wilson contracted seems to have been a real one, and not the 'diplomatic cold' John F Kennedy 'suffered' when he returned to Washington during the Cuban Missile Crisis, and it may well have had a significant impact on his resolve and morale – in the same recent historical model, it marks a definite turning point – but it was also a tactic and one which came off better in France than it did at home.

The French hid their anxiety with private jokes about Wilson running off home. Americans saw a tantrum that did not well become the country's president abroad. Tumulty was all in favour of confident stands as a way of building up public support, but he had to tell Wilson that this time his home audience was not impressed. When the President rejoined the Council of Four on 8 April, still unsteady, still in contact with the *George Washington*, he found that the Saar question was almost resolved – French ownership of the collieries, League of Nations supervision, and a plebiscite after a generation to determine either future independence, annexation by France or return to Germany – and Clemenceau, whose own health seemed shaky with a series of perhaps psychosomatic disorders, was almost prepared to run counter to Foch's strong insistence and agree to a temporary occupation of the Rhineland, with a carefully timetabled evacuation, also over 15 years. Lloyd George was in London when the French and Americans reached their agreement. He did not like it, but given that he had just enjoyed a parliamentary success at home, was better disposed to let it pass. Clemenceau promised

House that the French press would be kinder to Wilson again, and sure enough, in the last days of April, some of the old warmth returned.

One place where it seemed unlikely ever to return was Italy. Where less than six months ago, Wilson had been greeted like a Messiah, Americans were now warned to keep away from crowds, lest they be jostled and beaten. Wilson had committed himself in January 1918 to the adjustment of Italy's borders along *clearly recognisable lines of nationality*. This, however, conflicted with Italian claims to areas of the Adriatic coast which had been promised to them in the Treaty of London (which Wilson pretended he had never been shown), but to which they had subsequently added a claim on Fiume; Orlando's claim that Italy had title here because the bulk of the population was Italian-speaking led Wilson to joke that he hoped the prime minister wouldn't lay claim to parts of Manhattan on the same basis. Wilson was prepared to make a strategic exception in the case of the nearly quarter of a million German-speakers living in the Tyrol who would fall under Italian rule in order to guarantee her security in the northern passes, but the Yugoslavs on the Dalmatian coast represented a more sensitive case, and a real risk of future conflict. There could be no better illustration of the clash between the old system of secret diplomacy and the openness enjoined by the Fourteen Points, but the situation also illustrated Wilson's willingness to make pragmatic decisions with an eye to his standing at home, which was substantially improved by his strongly stated position: too strongly stated for the Italians, who following the President's statement of 23 April, walked out of the Conference for almost a fortnight.

The issue had a more general application, for if Wilson were to agree that Danzig be given to the Poles, as Clemenceau argued, he could not with any logic or consistency oppose Italy's claim to Fiume. Lloyd George proposed that Danzig be maintained as a free territory, which would still give Poland passage to the sea, but that borders should be settled along straightforwardly linguistic lines, narrowing the 'Polish corridor' to a degree that apparently reduced the charismatic Ignacy Paderewski, pianist and future prime minister of independent Poland, to tears.

He was not the only leader reduced to weeping. When Orlando could make no further headway against the other members of the Council of Four, he broke down and wept. The British were disgusted to hear of this, but Wilson showed compassion, a measure of the strange closeness that had developed between these unlikely sharers in the project of remaking a shattered world. Wilson and Clemenceau grew closer personally even as their political views diverged, and Lloyd George seemed to revel in the experience, later referring to his time in France as the happiest and most fulfilling of his life. Though the Four were mostly locked away *in camera* and without the benefit of minutes much of the time, which often led to disagreement over what had actually been discussed and decided, they were also subject to a steady flow of representations from national groups. This had been happening since the start of the Conference, sometimes to dramatic effect, as when Queen Marie of Romania arrived with much of her court and most of her dresses to lay claim to much of Hungary; that country went quietly Bolshevik in late March, though when the thunderclap did reach Paris there was immediate anxiety, fuelled by the appearance of short-lived Soviets elsewhere, that here was a greater challenge to the Fourteen Points even than a resurgent Germany: world revolution. Sometimes the approach was more circumspect, as when the Belgians started to insist on being heard. Their implicit refusal to sign any treaty coincided awkwardly with the Italian withdrawal and lent their claims considerably more weight. The timing was doubly awkward in that the German delegates had been summoned to Paris to receive terms and were expected imminently.

The day after Orlando's breakdown, Wilson showed Clemenceau and Lloyd George the statement he had prepared on the Italian question, typed out on his battered portable. It was published two days after that. Orlando and Sonnino were furious that the American president should have made what amounted to a direct appeal to the Italian people, but they were also aware that it made a direct appeal to the American people as well, and they tried to temporise, knowing that Wilson had only a year and a half of his administration left to run. In the event, Orlando was ousted from office, leaving Sonnino, a dour Protestant liberal whose hardening views had initially led him to favour alliance with the Central Powers rather than the Allies, to complete formalities on the treaty. Orlando later took pride in the fact that he was not a signatory. It was not until 1920, and following the operatic adventures of Gabriele d'Annunzio in Fiume, that the Adriatic situation was resolved.

The three (for the moment) remaining members of the Council of Four looked on Italy and Italian ways with deep ambivalence. Its politics seemed compounded of socialism and popery, a view which would have united Clemenceau (no lover of priests and popes), the non-conformist Lloyd George and the Presbyterian-liberal Wilson. Their views, Clemenceau's in particular, of the Japanese delegation were even more stereotyped. Japanese delegates, whose very presence at the conference seemed to some to be questionable, were treated with scant courtesy and when the Council of Ten was dissolved the Japanese – who like Italy were in Paris to secure specific demands but were not much interested in the broader aims of the Conference – were quietly dropped from the new body on the grounds that they had not sent a head of state (inconceivable in any case) or prime minister to the Conference. However, a specifically Japanese issue presented the next great challenge to Wilson's new world order and a further example of the clash between old and new diplomacy.

During the war, which Japan joined on the Allied side specifically in order to capture Germany's interests in the Far East, she had taken possession of Shandong province in China and imposed a treaty that recognised her claims. This clearly violated the self-determination of the Chinese, who made a poignant representation in Paris (as did the Koreans, who had been annexed in 1910) and it also threatened the sterling work of American Presbyterian missionaries who had been making striking progress in China. Japan, though, demanded that the Allies honour the 1917 agreement which promised her Shandong. Fearing a white alliance against the yellow races, and conscious that her own rapidly expanding overseas and international associations (including a naval alliance with the UK) made her ironically more vulnerable than she had been in the days of cultural and economic isolation, Japan also insisted that the League Covenant contain a clause which asserted full racial equality, something which neither Britain and the Dominions nor Woodrow Wilson was likely to grant. Though they must have recognised in it strong echoes of their own hemispheric concerns and recent history – rapid industrial growth, heightened overseas involvement, need to police near neighbours – the American delegates prepared a strong statement opposing the Japanese claim, but with the Conference precariously poised Wilson was obliged to compromise, giving the Japanese full economic rights in Shandong on the basis of an eventual withdrawal, which happened three years later after the Washington naval conference. Lansing's skills in international law came into their own on the issue, though it was the oratory of Wellington Koo, the youthful and charismatic Chinese ambassador to Washington, which made the biggest impact at the discussions. The settlement was fiercely opposed in America, where the Open Door policy came second only to the Monroe Doctrine as a sacrosanct principle, and Wilson's reputation, enhanced by his strong stand against Italy, was once again damaged. Though he was by now a marginal figure, Lansing was horrified by Wilson's compromise, and Tasker Bliss wrote a dissenting opinion; some younger members of the American delegation resigned on principle. The real damage, though, would only become evident when Wilson returned home to defend the peace settlement. Republicans – who mostly cared not a jot about the Chinese people or their rights – found the 'rape of Shandong' a useful stick for beating Wilson and his treaty and were happy to see the 'dagger pointed at the heart of China' turned against the League and its great proponent. Almost no other issue was so insistently raised in the chorus of opposition that greeted Wilson on his return. Few Americans really care who owned or administered Shandong, but Wilson's enemies detected an exploitable moment of weakness in his compromise on the issue.

By the end of the negotiations, wearied and frustrated, and in great physical discomfort, it looked very much as though Wilson, caught between the countervailing interests of Britain and France, was prepared to consider almost any revision that might guarantee and expedite a signable treaty. He strongly

III

The Legacy

7

Dare we break the heart of the world?

The elements of the Treaty of Versailles were extraordinarily various, some clear, some less so, many of them principled, as many fudged; there were inconsistencies and compromises, gains and disappointments; an overall sense that an entire philosophy had been trimmed and jostled in order to fit an ungeneralisable set of events and exponentially changing circumstances, but yet had more or less survived the process. In a remarkably short and concentrated effort, a huge amount of negotiation and drafting had been done by committees large and small. Since December 1918, fingers had been pointed in explanation or reinforcement of unprecedented ideas, wagged reproachfully or jabbed in anger. Now, with unexpected suddenness, they came together in a fist.

Even those responsible for the creation of the Treaty were surprised at its severity, which would leave Germany newly delimited, stripped of approximately one-tenth of her population, policed rather than defended by an army too small for her land-mass, bereft of colonies and in massive debt to some – but not all, which was the rub for the likes of England's

NORWAY
Kristiania
North Sea
IRISH FREE STATE
Dublin
UNITED KINGDOM OF GREAT BRITAIN AND NORTHERN IRELAND
DENMARK
Copenhagen
NETHERLANDS
Amsterdam
London
Brussels
BELGIUM
RHINELAND
GERMANY
LUXEMBOURG
SAAR
Paris
FRANCE
SWITZERLAND
AUSTRIA
Milan
ITALY
PORTUGAL
Lisbon
Madrid
ANDORRA
SPAIN
Rome
SPANISH MOROCCO
Mediterranean Sea
MOROCCO
ALGERIA
TUNISIA
0 500 kilometres

Europe 1923
FINLAND
Petrograd (St Petersburg)
Tallinn
ESTONIA
Riga
LATVIA
LITHUANIA
Vilnius
Königsberg
EAST PRUSSIA
Moscow
UNION OF SOVIET SOCIALIST REPUBLICS
Warsaw
Brest-Litovsk
POLAND
Kiev
Odessa
ROMANIA
Bucharest
Belgrade
BULGARIA
Sofia
Black Sea
Istanbul
TURKEY
GREECE
Athens
IRAQ
SYRIA
CYPRUS

oldest ally, the Portuguese – of her conquerors. Clemenceau probably came closest to the truth when he described it as a human document and therefore imperfect. Strangely, though, two men with whom he had spent the previous few months arguing, sometimes falling out, but the while forming a strange kind of friendship and fellow-feeling, seemed – but only seemed – to have reversed positions on the treaty. Wilson thought it was just, and in keeping with Germany's culpability, though viewed from whatever distance and with whatever political lens it seemed a long way removed from *peace without victory* and an unwillingness to discuss the sufficient and circumstantial causes of the war, just the general and abstract ones that created its necessary condition and could never be allowed to again. Once embarked on war, Wilson prosecuted it with unwavering determination and he took the same spirit into the peace, confident to the last that his League would mitigate any 'human error' that crept into the settlement. By contrast, Lloyd George, who had started out politically as a pacifist and ended the war demanding the sternest retribution for Germany, was having some second thoughts. He continued to worry that the Treaty put France in the ascendant in Western Europe, but his main concern was almost practical: his cabinet was not convinced that Germany would sign the Treaty; if Germany did not, the Allies would be required to resume the war; the British parliament and people could not countenance that possibility; therefore, the treaty needed to be changed.

What is most striking is not that these feelings should have emerged as that they should have emerged so dramatically with the publication of the treaty draft. The Germans were given minimal time to translate, read, absorb and respond to a treaty that had been handed to them in a single copy and in a language other than their own, a detail that is often adduced to underline the unilateral cruelty of the Treaty of Versailles. But others were in the same position. The Council of Four ordered the printing of the Treaty on 4 May, but finished copies were not available when the delegates were called together to vote on the terms. Instead, the entire text was read aloud by a member of the French delegation. When the Treaty did return, printed and bound, Wilson commented that he hoped he might be granted the leisure in years to come to read the whole thing.

Many of those who did were shocked by it. Keynes was already convinced that the economic consequences of the peace (he finished his essay of that name in what reads perversely like white-hot disillusionment and published it before the end of the year) would be disastrous; he described the terms as 'Carthaginian' and had resigned from the Treasury and left Paris before the signing. Jan Smuts begged Wilson to reconsider the treaty and make it more reasonable, as did Herbert Hoover. The three men famously met in the pre-dawn of 7 May, called from sleep by the arrival of the printed version of the Treaty, left sleepless by its content and tone. Others in the American delegation, including William Bullitt, were shocked enough to resign. Such reactions may seem ill-timed, even inconsistent, but they were the result of reading the document as a whole, rather than considering its content item by item, in separate committees, over a period of many weeks. Text also has a way of setting out ideas with unambiguous coldness and clarity. The most contentious, which Germany had been fearing but hoping might be minimised, was the infamous Article 231, which laid the charge of war guilt.

The Germans had, of course, been holding their own councils on the peace terms. They had accepted the armistice on the basis that no colonies would be seized, no reparations pursued other than a reasonable war indemnity, and that the principle of self-determination guaranteed by Wilson would apply as much to German-speakers in Eastern Europe and Alsace-Lorraine as to Poles, Czechs and Hungarians. A certain amount of back-channel diplomacy had left the Germans believing that France was willing to offer concessions in Silesia (*bien entendu!* Silesia was far from France), in return for the Saar coalfield. Above all, the Germans believed that Wilson and the Americans would guarantee a fair settlement and that Wilson's apparent lack of interest in belabouring matters of guilt might mean that the question of culpability for the war be set aside.

The German delegation arrived in Paris on 29 April. Their train had been made to travel slowly through the battlefields of the Western Front, as if to provide a bracing jolt to a people who, like the French, had reacted to war's end with an outbreak of myopic hedonism and self-centred fantasy: despite real and bloody conflict within Germany, much of the 'revolutionary'spirit that ran through the defeated country in 1918, has a playful, substanceless, sensuous aspect that came out again in 'Weimar' politic and culture and which foreshadows the spirit of the student riots, largely sparked by the Vietnam War, that spread across Europe 50 years later. A similar spirit was evident in Paris in 1918; the difference was that the French had 'won' (though not quite yet, both Clemenceau and Foch believed, with their different solutions) and the French already had one hand on a peace treaty. The German delegation was brusquely deposited at Versailles but well enough treated in Paris and there seem to have been no murderous assaults. The delegation was headed by the German foreign minister Count Ulrich von

Brockdorff-Rantzau, who for all his wartime enthusiasm for a negotiated peace managed to look like the archetypal scion of Prussian militarism. Some suggested that his refusal to stand when the terms were presented was simple inability, given his alleged taste for vintage champagne and cocaine; it was intended to show that the delegation and Germany herself were not in the dock; the Allied leaders read it as disrespect and defiance, but they already knew what Germany was being 'offered'.

The Germans were summoned to the Trianon Palace Hotel on 7 May. Brockdorff-Rantzau had apparently written a second, briefer and more conciliatory speech for the occasion, but the one he read enraged and disgusted the men opposite him. Clemenceau and Lloyd George had expected some kind of contrition; in his fury at the defiant and self-justifying German speech, which seems to have been crudely and ineptly translated, the British prime minister apparently snapped in half an elegant paper knife he had been toying with. The Germans, in their turn and when they had been given a chance actually to read the Treaty, were disgusted and angry with Wilson, who they felt had betrayed every promise enshrined in the Fourteen Points and had turned as vengeful as the Allied leaders. Article 231 was the distillation of treachery, but it was also a blank cheque; admission of war guilt meant that Germany could reasonably expect to face any punishment the Allies set down, so it was on this question that much of the German response centred.

The terms were, of course, rejected. In a frantic bout of activity, a set of counter-proposals were drafted and despatched. The French orchestrated disturbances in the Rhineland to underline the validity of France's anxieties and its claims. Lloyd George found that the mood in Britain had become more conciliatory towards Germany and that talk of pips squeaking was no longer politically useful. He disgusted Wilson by insisting on change in the very clauses he had formerly endorsed so fiercely. The British Empire delegation felt that the Treaty was entirely French in tendency and threatened economic disaster by destroying Germany. Wilson's impatient insistence that the Germans pay a heavy price for the war carried the day in renewed discussions on the reparations question. The Treaty was presented to Germany again with those clauses intact and unrevised, but this time with a deadline that carried the specific threat of renewed armed force. The only hint of conciliation was a three-day extension to the deadline, though that may have been to give Foch time to assemble his weary soldiery for the decisive strike he – if not they – wished to unleash at the foe.

The foe was already in deep confusion. Brockdorff-Rantzau, perhaps investing too much faith in his own rhetoric, believed that the treaty was a bluff and that a resolute and united Germany could secure advantageous – or, rather, damage-limiting – changes. Others argued that signing now would at least allow Germany to stabilise, regroup economically and eliminate the threat of Bolshevism. At the eleventh hour, Friedrich Ebert managed to form a new government in Weimar and at the second attempt to push through acceptance of all the terms, including Article 231. The message arrived late enough in Paris for Clemenceau to have to hold off celebration in order to cancel Foch's invasion orders. How frustrated the old soldier must have been.

Two days before, on 21 June, the German High Seas Fleet had scuttled itself in Scapa Flow where it had been interned after the Armistice, an act that preserved some vestige of German military honour, embarrassed the Royal Navy and consequently amused the Americans, but also guaranteed that there would be no further extension of the deadline. It was an expensive act of defiance, undertaken in part to camouflage Germany's own embarrassment at the filthy, mutinous state of her formerly proud and technically undefeated navy.

The date chosen for the handing over of terms to Germany had coincided, deliberately or coincidentally isn't clear, with one of that same navy's more infamous moment. May 7th 1919 was the fourth anniversary of the sinking of the *Lusitania*. A more obviously symbolic date was chosen for the signing of the treaty. June 28th was the fifth anniversary of the Sarajevo assassinations. The Allies spent the morning firming up their 'Association' with the United States, putting on paper a mutual defence agreement that neither House nor Wilson believed would pass Congress. They were then taken by car to Versailles where the carpets had been hastily repaired and the mirrors polished in the great Galerie des Glaces.

William Orpen's painting of the signing is a historical icon rather than a realistic representation of what was in any case a media event, every conceivable vantage at Versailles being taken up by a camera. The canvas shows Wilson, handsomer and more potent than he was by this stage, holding the treaty, the only one of the Allied and Associated leaders who seems at this moment to be engaging with the text. Wilson and Clemenceau, though now ostensibly close friends, almost have their backs turned to one another. The French prime minister, who thought this a great day for France, looks stony and remote, not at all the 'scrunched homunculus' described by Harold Nicholson.[1] Lloyd George is inscrutable. In front of them, almost overlooked, like the victims in an *auto-da-fé*, are the German signatories, Dr Müller standing solicitously over the bowed figure of Dr Bell. Above their heads, the slightly misaligned mirrors give back the warped grid of the window-frames giving what is clearly intended as a triumphal image a measure of ambivalence and uncertainty. This is how the world will look henceforward, it seems to say, the old geographies giving place to a strange new geometry.

That evening, accompanied by Clemenceau, who seemed unwilling to part with the man who had arguably delivered him the treaty he and France wanted, Wilson left for Le Havre and home. In a last conversation with Edward House, and it was to be the very last, Wilson told him that the only things in life worth having were those that were worth fighting over. The remark has been seen as a further rebuke to House over his concessions to the Allies during Wilson's absence from Paris, but in suggesting that House might have fought harder for things and that he would not take the Treaty to the Senate in anything other than a forceful and unconciliatory way it also re-asserts Wilson's belief that victory and rightness were somehow mutually reinforcing. In fighting for what one believes to be right, one makes it more right, and more right still when one wins the fight.

Let us avoid acting in a manner which would risk creating sympathies for Germany; neither let us seek to interpret our promises with a lawyer's finesse.
WOODROW WILSON

This was not the kind of logic or psychology that was going to thrive in the United States in 1919. Wilson's whole intellectual project was premised on the essential goodness of human nature; evil was simply a matter of maladjustment in human affairs, remedied by eliminating secrecy and naked self-interest. In contrast, the European leaders with whom he negotiated and the politicians at home who remained unpersuaded of his League and the Treaty that depended on it regarded evil as, if not absolute, then at least a convenient descriptor for any interest that did not square with their own. One ironic outcome of Wilson's philosophical confidence was that it made him deeply intolerant of anyone who did not automatically share his view. Negotiation was, in a sense, alien to his nature, though he willingly countenanced concessions and compromises that still unambiguously delivered his desired ends.

In early 1919, the increasingly estranged House counselled Wilson that negotiation with Henry Cabot Lodge was the only course that would deliver ratification of the Treaty. Wilson's intractability, though, was compounded by what might well have been jealousy of the highly educated Lodge's domestic reputation as an intellectual. Not only did he dislike the idea of negotiation on what seemed self-evident truths, he feared exposing his own thinking to Lodge's critical faculties. Apart from the squabble over the location of a graduate school at Princeton, Wilson was used to winning; perhaps he lacked a measure of the occasional loser's realism. The result was a stalemate of disengagement, considerably more damaging to Wilson's cause than a measure of negotiation and compromise would have been. On the other hand, his obduracy over the League and insistence that the Covenant be accepted whole and unqualified had considerable logic. Tumulty, who monitored the situation at home, convinced the president that there was sufficient public and congressional support for the League to ensure ratification.

The Republican party was substantially divided over the League, though the number of irreconcilable opponents was actually quite small. Between those heartily in favour, who included senator Porter J McCumber of North Dakota and ex-President Taft, and those, like the highly vocal William

E Borah of Idaho and the splendidly named and deceptively brilliant Philander C Knox of Pennsylvania, who opposed the League in any shape or form as a wholesale abandonment of America's traditional isolationism, there was a spectrum of Republican opinion that accepted the worth of the League, but only with qualifications that served American interests on the international stage rather than the utopian internationalism, as they saw it, of Wilson's model. When he presented the Covenant to the Senate on 10 July, Wilson asked rhetorically, *Dare we break the heart of the world?*[2] The reply which lay in wait for him, once Lodge had marshalled his opposition, was that Wilson had already broken hearts and was fated to as long as he continued the un-American practice of involving himself and his country in other peoples' concerns. The impression given was of a small boy who despite repeated warnings pokes his stick into a wasps' nest – some right-wing opinion of Europe, the Middle East and Asia was no more elevated than that – only to find he is stung and has inflicted stings on others.

Lodge had secured a Republican majority in the Senate Foreign Relations Committee, which gave him considerable leverage. His tactics depended on a series of shrewd guesses and assumptions. Lodge believed that simple delay would damage pro-League support, which had a whiff of post-war euphoria about it. He could also assume that those who supported the League in principle but would only ratify if specifically American interests were safeguarded, would not trade or compromise on that position. Of particular concern, beyond the preservation of the Monroe Doctrine as a more than regional understanding was the prospect of the United States' one vote being ranged against the seven of Britain and the Dominions. This was, of course, to confuse assembly and council votes, and to ignore the fact that semi-autonomous territories under American control would also have votes. Next, and in the event most damagingly, Lodge counted on Wilson, a party man as well as a principled one, having no truck with the 'Mild Reservationists' who required minor and essentially undamaging changes to the Covenant. That is, and again the guess was correct, he counted on Wilson himself to destroy his 'own' creation. Finally, Lodge could count on his own enormous personal authority – he was known as 'the ambassador from Massachusetts to the United States' – to solidify anti-League feeling.

He did, however, have the means to orchestrate that feeling. The Senate hearings into the League Covenant were a curious mixture of good political theatre and subtle farce. When the draft Treaty was presented to the Allies in Paris, Clemenceau's assistant André Tardieu read out a summary in advance of the printed version arriving. Though the Covenant was readily available to all interested parties, Lodge insisted on reading out the entire document, a process which sowed in some American minds the impression that a country, which had been born in and thrived under a crisp and mnemonic statement of principles was in danger of committing itself to vaguely worded promises and potentially damaging involvements. The reading occupied an entire fortnight, though few stayed to listen. The public hearings that followed were more interesting, not least in that they offered Senators, most of whom, even on the Foreign Relations Committee, had only the sketchiest idea of events and conditions abroad, a crash course in world politics. The most damaging contributions, as Lodge had hoped, came from pro-Chinese speakers. The betrayal of Shandong levelled a hard question at Wilson, but also raised the question of whether there had been unanimity in the American delegation, with the implicit question of whether Wilson had behaved dictatorially and ignored informed counsels. There was also the apparent inconsistency of his refusal to support Irish nationalism which had been (and continued to be) bloodily suppressed. If the Chinese-American lobby was relatively small, the underlying principle was not. The Irish-American community was not small and commanded considerable political weight. There was also a tide of anti-British and anti-French feeling, spurred by the suggestion that American troops had made only a minimal contribution to the fighting, and that the Allies had won the war alone. This was particularly inflammatory at a moment when America was still sending food and money to support both economies.

Wilson did not want to appear intransigent. He agreed to make public some of the commissioners' views, though at Tumulty's insistence, not those relating to the Shandong decision, and on 19 August he even agreed to be questioned by the committee at the White House, the only time an incumbent president has ever done so. The appearance was characteristic of Wilson's belief that faced with small groups of men, he could always exert sufficient persuasion to carry an argument. Unfortunately, on this occasion there was a growing group who baulked at any suggestion that League membership would require America to take action if any fellow-member were attacked or interfered with. Wilson made it clear that Article X of the Covenant was there at his insistence and that the document as a whole was indissoluble. He could listen to objections, but he would not and could not, and this was absolutely correct, entertain revisions without returning the Covenant to the other signatories, and without involving Germany. Wilson also lied to the committee, as some of those present must have realised, in stating that he had no knowledge of secret wartime treaties among the Allies.

The committee appearance was perhaps an even greater and more damaging misjudgement than the fateful speaking tour to the West and Midwest that began just over two weeks later. It strongly reinforced a suspicion that the League, rather than the expression of an estimable liberal ideal, was the President's own hobby-horse, and that he was increasingly isolated even from his own cabinet and fellow-commissioners. The public hearings had done a subtler form of damage to the League as well, entertaining a procession of witnesses – the testimony rose to nearly 1,300 pages – whose claim to speak for a particular national or ethnic group was often strongly questionable and whose points were often irrelevant, creating an impression of the League as a Babel of self-interest. There was also some attempt to point up how African-Americans had fared under a Southern Democrat president. There was still strong support for the idea of free black republics in Africa – and support from both sides of the colour line – but it was clear that the principle of self-determination would not stretch to the state of Georgia. The question had not arisen, but the League's Republican opponents were happy to exploit any perceived contradiction.

Following his stroke in October 1919, Wilson retreated into an 'Olympian seclusion'. At noon on 19 November 1919, just over a year after the end of the war, Senate convened to vote on the Treaty. Lodge now had strong backing for his Fourteen Reservations, cleverly numbered so as to suggest the Fourteen Points. The acting Democratic minority leader Gilbert M Hitchcock of Nebraska mishandled a well-intentioned attempt to save the League with only 'mild' – that is, largely interpretative – reservations. The 'Mild

Reservationists' had moved over to Lodge's camp. Wilson had received representations from his old 'war cabinet' ally and devoted friend Bernard Baruch to accept the Lodge reservations as the price of winning ratification for the League, and from Herbert Hoover, who believed that peace was more important than politics. Ailing and querulous, Wilson considered both men to have betrayed him. He instructed Democrats to vote against a qualified Treaty. Some disobeyed, but the Treaty with Lodge's reservations was defeated 55 votes to 39, with Democrats and 'Irreconcilables' voting together. Hitchcock tried to force an adjournment, but lost; this time the 'Irreconcilables' voted with the Republicans. There were further votes, on the Treaty with Hitchcock's 'Mild Reservations' and then, because Lodge knew he had nothing to fear, a vote on the Treaty as it stood, and as Wilson wished to see it passed. The measure only won 38 votes, with half a dozen Democrats defecting.

Four months later there was a last vote on the Treaty. Back-channel discussion had revealed the British would not raise fundamental objections to a clause which preserved the Monroe Doctrine and had reassured doubters on the question of Dominion votes as against a single American vote in the Assembly. Wilson was by now losing grip on his own party, who in a presidential election year had other priorities. As the Republic senator Frank B Brandegee of Connecticut sourly commented, 'We can always depend on Mr Wilson. He never has failed us'.[3] Though even at this late and seemingly terminal stage, the President would not budge, 21 Democrats defied him and voted for the Treaty with the Lodge reservations. Wilson loyalists and 'Irreconcilables' again voted together, but the final count of 49–35 fell seven votes short of the two-thirds majority required to pass. The result suggested that even in his decline and even at a moment when party interest outweighed other concerns, Wilson still had devoted personal support even as he rocked his own brainchild to death. The United States was required to make a separate peace with Germany and never became a member of the League of Nations.

ooooo

When Woodrow Wilson died on 3 February 1924, the German embassy in Washington failed to lower its flag as a mark of respect. In the opinion of most Germans, Wilson had abandoned them to the vengeful French and gone back on the guarantees he had offered in the Fourteen Points. Revisionist or 'realist' historians have gone some way toward arguing that the Versailles Treaty was not as damaging to Germany as the consensus view – most urgently summed up in its moral as well as economic aspects by John Maynard Keynes – might suggest. For a start, Germany was not dismembered. Had the principle of self-determination been applied to Bavaria, where there was a small but vocal separatist lobby and where a matter of days after Wilson's death a former Austrian corporal in the Germany army began dictating the personal testament and manifesto he titled *Mein Kampf*, the measure might have been considered. As it was, the creation of an independent Hungary – where the revolution could be usefully spun as nationalist rather than Communist – and even more contentiously of an independent Poland offered Germany a powerful *cordon* against the Soviet Union and reduced the spectre (ironically enough, in the circumstances) of another war on two fronts. In addition, the figure set in 1921 for reparations of 132 billion marks (the equivalent of more than £6.5 billion) was offset by some repayments already, fudged through a system of bond, defaulted by Germany, and then steadily run down and forgotten. France received considerably less from Germany between 1921 and Hitler's rise to power than Germany had taken from France after 1871. German industry had been left virtually intact and her leaders quickly learned that many provisions of the Treaty could be flouted without undue risk if not quite with impunity.

The prevailing and persistent view that the Treaty of Versailles simply marked an extended armistice in a continuous European conflict retains some justice, but it also overlooks profound changes in geopolitics and in military technology. The Second World War was different in kind from the First in that the rise of two continental superpowers, the Soviet Union and the United States, had replace the old European empires as the centres of economic, military, ideological and cultural influence and also because the rapid rise of military aviation and other forms of mechanisation changed the nature of warfare itself. The casually moralistic assertion that the world had not 'learned the lessons' of the First World War tended to ignore the obvious fact that some of those lessons were no longer applicable by 1939.

That the League of Nations failed is not in doubt. That its failure was in some part precipitated by America's refusal to join is beyond argument. It stands now as a kind of noble irrelevance, little researched (though richly dramatised by the Australian novelist Frank Moorhouse) and not much admired even for its idealism. To what extent Woodrow Wilson is responsible for that failure and to what extent the demise of the League confirmed *his* failure is a more complex question. Wilson's own temperamental complexities are more apparent than actual and often evaporate on closer examination. The best argument against any view of his mission as an essentially Christian one is how determinedly this-worldly and actual – in the sense of present and immediate – his politics were. In his 1890 essay 'Leaders of Men' Wilson had argued against the politics of posterity, the kind of idealism that delivers benefits of hindsight to the next generation. His personal faith seems to have been precisely that, and only loosely connected to a liberalism that was thoroughly secular in both principle and practice. The apparent pietism of his speeches is actually significantly less than that of many of his predecessors and successors.

Wilson's intellectual armature was the practice of politics itself. It was both his greatest strength and his most insidious weakness that the making of specific policy interested him significantly less than the nature and exercise of political power. In striving to make America a beacon for the world's nations, Wilson actually turned the American presidency into the bellwether of global politics, a role grasped and practised with different emphases and in very different contexts by Franklin Roosevelt, Harry Truman, Dwight Eisenhower, John F Kennedy, Richard Nixon (and Gerald Ford), Jimmy Carter, Ronald Reagan, Bill Clinton and both George H W Bush and George W Bush. If his own comment about the 'irony of fate' suggests a discontinuity between his first and second administrations, that too is misleading, for Wilson's domestic reforms between 1912 and 1916 were all of a sort to allow America to act on the world stage as an equal partner and strong competitor to the 'traditional' powers of Europe. The exact circumstances of his involvement in world affairs could not have been predicted, and required a fairly considerable revision of his original aims, but there is no reason to present Wilson as a man thrust unwillingly into international affairs.

Like most Americans of his generation, he was only inadequately versed in the realities of the non-American world and his comments and behaviour even in Paris revealed a level of ignorance – he seemed initially unsure where Fiume was and what its allegiances might be – and of prejudicial thinking about other cultures, particularly those from the non-Anglo-Saxon races. But it has to be remembered that the Paris peace negotiations only occupied six months of his 63 years to date, and that the First World War, even dated from Sarajevo rather than America's entry into it, or even the sinking of the *Lusitania*, only occupied half of his national political career. It is somewhat remarkable that a man who had reached the age of 54 without any involvement in electoral politics should have been identified not just as *a* world leader, but for many on both sides of the conflict as *the* world leader less than a decade later.

Wilson's claim as a maker of the modern world hinges less on what he did at Paris and far less than commonly supposed on the idea of the League of Nations, to which Sir Edward Grey and even Theodore Roosevelt lay some claim, and more on what he did to modernise and reposition the American presidency and to do so without overt constitutional reform. Wilson had made a significant impact before becoming New Jersey governor as a writer and man of ideas. To describe his approach to politics as visionary is not simply to highlight its utopian aspect – the abolition of war, the mucking-out of the Augean stables of diplomatic secrecy, the spread of representative democracy to all parts of the globe, all of which can be seen as a kind of Americanism-writ-large – but in the very fact that he regarded the art of politics as the marshalling of population behind a specific vision and the art of leadership as an embrace of whatever contingency was required to maintain that vision intact. Wilson was an evolutionist. The very root of his pragmatism was the belief that once an idea or a principle was given light and air, it would begin to interact with reality, present need, other potentially competing principles and would behave in the most straightforward way like a living organism. To expect any great idea to emerge complete and fully functioning, an imago that had never gone through the larval stage, was to Wilson foolish naivety. To wait until it was advanced enough for self-sustenance was to miss the necessary moment.

This is what is behind Wilson's apparent intractability in 1919. It was to be his vision of the League or no vision of the League, and without Wilson's pragmatism as well as his idealism a reduced League was fated to fail. Whether America, which by 1919 had become the world's banker as well as its most powerful manufacturing economy, suffered from its self-exclusion is harder to determine. Wilson himself believed that by taking charge of the peace he could enhance America's economic and political influence on the rest of the world. It was not merely a selfless and universalising project but a distinctively American and self-interested one. On the positive side, the experience of war in Europe rapidly professionalised and modernised the United States' foreign service. Even if some of Robert Lansing's work failed to rise above the non-obvious, certainly from the perspective of the European powers, it did much to bring America up to speed with the rest of the world. However, as with Japan's 'opening' and modernisation, the rate of change significantly warped some elements of the process, leading to repressive practices at home (born of a morbid suspicion of foreignness) and an incurable addiction to the very forms of secrecy that Wilson had set out to combat among other nations. A future American secretary of state, John Foster Dulles, was one of those who helped draft the notorious Article 231 on German war guilt; Dulles's brother Allan was the first director of the Central Intelligence Agency. Perhaps something of their 'Cold War' world view was formed in the embers of 1918.

The broader question of what were the implications of the United States' failure to join the League of Nations is not susceptible of an easy or single answer. Clearly, the decision had more evident impact on the League than it did on the United States, weakening it considerably and robbing it of both the moral force and the irresistible economic and even military authority America could have brought to future disputes. In America's absence, the League tended to default to the old, pre-war European culture of *sub rosa* agreements and secret diplomacy rather than the open discussion Wilson considered a basic imperative in modern world politics.

The United States' self-exclusion from the League did, at one level, represent a reversal of the expansionist spirit that had been instilled after 1898. After hosting the Washington Treaties, that attempted to stabilise the Far East, America again withdrew from world affairs. Post-war prosperity made this a logical and largely unproblematic stance until the crash of 1929 and increasingly volatile politics in Asia and Europe enforced a change of attitude. In 1930 and 1931, Republican Secretary of State Henry L Stimson attended the London Naval Conference, led a delegation to a disarmament conference in Geneva and issued the so-called 'Stimson Doctrine', opposing Japanese aggression in Manchuria. None of these initiatives gained significant public support at home, a clear indication of the gap between popular indifference to foreign policy and governmental recognition that America's position in a new world order had to be actively maintained.

Nevertheless, between 1935 and 1937 the country responded to crises in Abyssinia, in the Rhineland and again in China, by ratifying a series of Neutrality Acts that prohibited loans, the sales of arms and other materiel, and denied credit on any non-military sales to belligerent countries. There was even an attempt to safeguard against the dilemmas presented by the *Falaba*, *Arabic*, *Lusitania* and *Sussex* sinkings by preventing Americans from embarking on vessels owned by belligerent powers.

On the other hand, Wilsonian diplomacy had seen the liberal-progressive ideal enacted in an unprecedented international situation which significantly compromised its independence of action and its moral purism. The war turned America into the world's largest trading nation, both in cash and commodities, and the rise of neo-imperialistic Bolshevism in Russia created the very real and immediate spectre of a two-superpower confrontation, which even in a pre-nuclear age, significantly affected the hemispheric politics of the Monroe Doctrine. It is significant that at the beginning of the Second World War, Congress quickly revised the Neutrality Acts to allow (as in 1915) financial and trade assistance to the UK.

Between 1914 and 1939, Wilson's beacon of light was transformed into Franklin Roosevelt's 'arsenal of democracy' and this represented a net and, to date, permanent change in America's overseas disposition. The 'irony of fate' was of a circumstantial sort, but it changed America and arguably reversed some of the democratising initiatives of the Progressive Era by removing elements of foreign policy from public scrutiny – where entanglement was still unpopular – and leaving much of it vested in the executive branch and in a network of secret or semi-secret bodies, later most notoriously the Central Intelligence Agency, which had a specifically non-domestic remit. Of such is conspiracy theory born; the very principle that Wilson had identified as the root of all international ills was quickened again at the heart of the American polity.

ooooo

Wilson has suffered disproportionately from the kind of casual revisionism that takes its energy from purely psychological and emotional (or in his case, medical) concerns. There is no need to see Woodrow Wilson as leading a country while battling personal demons, nor to believe that some of his most important decisions were taken while in pain or suffering from depression. That not only belittles the man; it degrades the achievement. Wilson was frequently resistant to collective wisdom or to common counsel, but less often than is sometimes suggested, and only ever when either led him and the United States away from his fixed goal. For Wilson, peace and democracy were not neutral qualities but active forces that had to be fuelled, maintained and protected with considerable determination and rigour. He expended so much of those qualities during his six months in Paris that there was little left when he returned to America. He compounded the problem by going to the country in emulation of his political idols. A hale and hearty Wilson in November 1919 might have exercised sufficient personal authority to win over the reservationists. Wilson attracts counterfactual speculation more often than any other American president precisely because his career is so criss-crossed with alternative eventualities. His two presidential election victories were close enough to suggest a forking of the historical path.

Would Theodore Roosevelt have taken the country to war in 1914 or as soon as American lives were lost? If Wilson had not gained the White House until 1916, on an anti-war ticket or otherwise, would he as only a first-term president had the impetus and the desire for re-election to carry through the League? The reality is that America entered the war as early as she reasonably could and that the rejection of the League was ultimately both a failure of imagination and an act of revenge by vested interests, anxious to rob Wilson of his glory and the Democratic party of an extended run in the White House. The psychology – or chronology – of liberalism and conservatism is usually misdescribed. Conservatives are less interested in the past than in present gain and stability. Liberals, like Woodrow Wilson, are less interested in the abstract future than in present justice and equity. It was in the present tense that Wilson and his opponents clashed on the terms of his great vision. It is one of the most remarkable political spectacles of modern times, not least in what it tells us about how the spectacle often outweighs the substance of politics. Wilson offered the world something new and rather extraordinary, a self-willed evolutionary leap into an era that might conceivably transcend the cycle of want and bloodshed that had characterised much of recorded history. That the world failed to follow through on his challenge is ultimately unsurprising, but the challenge, though defeated in the corridors of power, has never quite been erased and remains in force even today, to some extent in the United Nations, founded at the end of another world war and this time with American support and membership, but also as pure idea. The terms of international conflict may seem unprecedented but which have since the demise of the Soviet empire recovered a striking similarity to those of 1918, most notably in Iraq where

Notes

Introduction: *Dear Ghosts ...*

1. Thomas A Bailey, *Woodrow Wilson and the Great Betrayal* (New York: 1947) p 277.
2. Sigmund Freud and William C Bullitt, *Woodrow Wilson: A Psychological Study* (Boston, MA: 1967).
3. John Milton Cooper Jr, *The Warrior and the Priest: Woodrow Wilson and Theodore Roosevelt* (Cambridge, MA: 1983).
4. H W Brands, *Woodrow Wilson* (New York: 2003) p 1, hereafter Brands.
5. Arthur S Link and others (ed), *The Papers of Woodrow Wilson*, 69 volumes (Princeton, NJ: 1966–94), hereafter *PWW*.
6. Jan Willem Schulte Nordholt, *Woodrow Wilson: A Life for World Peace,* English edition (Berkeley, CA: 1991) p 8.
7. Hugh Brogan, *The Pelican History of the United States of America* (Harmondsworth: 1986) p 458, hereafter Brogan.

8. Full text online at www.firstworldwar/source/wilsonspeech_league.htm
9. *PWW,* Vol. 44, p 485.
10. 'Leaders of Men', June 1890, *PWW,* Vol. 10, p 646.
11. Cited Karl Nordstrom, 'Woodrow Wilson and Post-War America', unpublished thesis (Tromsø: 1983).
12. Frequently cited, but probably apocryphal.
13. Pueblo address, 25 September 1919; subsequent quotations from same source.
14. Randolph Bourne, 'War and the Intellectuals', in *War and the Intellectuals: Collected Essays* (NY: 1976) p 8.
15. Memo of 4 January 1918, *PWW,* Vol. 45, p 455.

1: *Exegetical* and *evangelical*

1. Cited in John A Thompson, *Woodrow Wilson* (London: 2002) p 134.
2. Full text and facsimile online at www.docsouth.unc/edu/imls/wilson.htm
3. Journal entry, 28 December 1889, *PWW*, Vol. 6, p 462.
4. Letter to John Leckie, ?4 July 1875, *PWW,* Vol. 2, p 98.
5. Cited in letter from Ellen Axson Wilson to Anna Harris, 12 February 1907, *PWW,* Vol. 17, p 35.
6. *PWW,* Vol. 1, p 308.
7. Letter from Wilson to Ellen Axson Wilson, 19 July 1902, *PWW,* Vol. 14, p 27.
8. Walter Bagehot, 'The Cabinet', *The English Constitution* (London: 1867) p 143.
9. Walter Bagehot, 'The Character of Sir Robert Peel', in *Biographical Studies* (London: 1881) p 94.
10. Letter to Robert Bridges, 29 April 1883, *PWW,* Vol. 2, p 343.

11. Letter to Robert Bridges, 19 November 1884, *PWW*, Vol. 2, p 465.
12. Woodrow Wilson, *Congressional Government: A Study in American Politics (*Boston: 1885) p 101, hereafter *Congressional Government.*
13. *PWW*, Vol. 2, p 499.

2: *God ordained ...*

1. *Congressional Government*, p 27.
2. Brogan, p 449.

3: *Too Proud to Fight*

1. Second inaugural address, 5 March 1917, *PWW*, Vol. 23, p 312.
2. Cited Ray Stannard Baker (ed.), *Woodrow Wilson: Life and Letters*, 8 volumes (Garden City, NY: 1927–9) Vol. 4, p 55.
3. Ambrose Bierce, *The Devil's Dictionary* (New York: 1911) p 148.
4. Sir Cecil Spring-Rice to Sir Edward Grey, 8 September 1914, *PWW*, Vol. 31, p 13.
5. Address to newly naturalised citizens, Philadelphia, 10 May 1915, *PWW*, Vol. 33, p 149.
6. Correspondence between Grey and House, 10 August 1915, *PWW*, Vol. 34, p 372.
7. Letter to William Jennings Bryan, 9 June 1915, *PWW*, Vol. 33, p 205.
8. Address to Senate, 22 January 1917, *PWW*, Vol. 40, p 536.
9. War Address to Congress, 2 April 1917, *PWW*, Vol. 41, p 526.

10. War Address to Congress, 2 April 1917, *PWW*, Vol. 41, pp 523–4.

4: *Force without stint or limit*

1. Admiral Eduard von Capelle to the Budget Committee of the Reichstag, 21 January 1917, cited by Arthur S Link, *Woodrow Wilson; Campaigns for Progressivism and Peace* (Princeton, NJ: 1965) p 246.
2. Speech in Baltimore, 6 April 1918, *PWW*, Vol. 46, p 200.
3. Cited in Margaret MacMillan, *The Peacemakers: Six Months That Changed the World* (London: 2001) p 167, hereafter MacMillan.
4. Sir William Wiseman memo, 16 August 1918, *PWW*, Vol. 49, p 274.
5. Diary of W C Bullitt, 10 December 1918, *PWW*, Vol. 53, p 352.
6. *PWW*, Vol. 49, p 345.
7. Robert Lansing, *The Peace Negotiations: A Personal Narrative* (Boston/NY: 1921) p 134, hereafter Lansing.

5: *America saved the world ...*

1. Edith Wharton, *Ethan Frome* (New York: 1911) p 14.
2. Letter to Mrs William James, 1 April 1913, in Leon Edel (ed), *Letters of Henry James* (New York: 1984) Vol. 4, p 619.
3. David Hunter Miller, *The Drafting of the Covenant*, 2 volumes (New York: 1928) Vol. 1, p 38.
4. John Maynard Keynes, *The Economic Consequences of the Peace* (London: 1919) p 24, hereafter Keynes.
5. Keynes, p 46.
6. Speech in Boston, 24 February 1919, *PWW*, Vol. 55, pp 240–5.

7. Cited in Thomas J Knock, *To End All Wars: Woodrow Wilson and the Quest for a New World Order* (New York: 2001) p 241.
8. Lansing, p 103.

6: *The present tides*

1. Speech to Democratic National Committee, 28 February 1919, cited Brands, p 109.
2. MacMillan, p 211.
3. MacMillan, p 347.

7: *Dare we break the heart of the world?*

1. Harold Nicholson, *Peacemaking, 1919* (London: 1924) p 230.
2. Speech to Senate, 19 July 1919, *PWW*, Vol. 60, p 424.
3. Cited in Thomas A Bailey, *Woodrow Wilson and the Great Betrayal* (NY: 1947) p 304.

Chronology

YEAR	AGE	THE LIFE AND THE LAND
1856		29 Dec: Born to Joseph Ruggles Wilson and Jessie Woodrow Wilson, at Staunton, VA.
1858	1/2	Family moves to Augusta, GA.
1860	3/4	Abraham Lincoln elected US President: Carolina secedes from the Union in protest.
1861	4/5	6 Jan: Joseph Ruggles co-founds breakaway Presbyterian Church of the United States, delivers sermon 'Mutual Relations of Masters and Slaves'. Outbreak of American Civil War.
1863	6/7	American Civil War: Confederate defeats at Gettysburg and Vicksburg; Lincoln's 'Gettysburg Address'; Confederate victory at Chickamauga.
1864	7/8	American Civil War: General Grant made Commander-in-Chief of Union Army; Lincoln re-elected; Sherman's march through Georgia.

	HISTORY	CULTURE
1856	Peace Conference in Paris recognises integrity of Ottoman Empire. Second Opium War begins.	Flaubert, *Madame Bovary*.
1858	End of Indian Mutiny. Suez Canal Company formed.	Thomas Carlyle, *Frederick the Great*.
1860	Garibaldi lands in Italy. Anglo-French troops reach Beijing.	Wilkie Collins, *The Woman in White*. George Eliot, *The Mill on the Floss*.
1861	Wilhelm I becomes King of Prussia. Italy declared a kingdom under Victor Emmanuel II of Sardinia. Death of Prince Albert.	Charles Dickens, *Great Expectations*. George Eliot, *Silas Marner*. Mrs Beeton, *Book of Household Management*.
1863	Schleswig incorporated into Denmark. French capture Mexico City. Construction of London Underground begins.	Charles Kingsley, *The Water Babies*. Football Association founded, London.
1864	Schleswig War: Austrian and Prussian troops defeat Danes. Archduke Maximilian of Austria crowned Emperor of Mexico.	Charles Dickens, *Our Mutual Friend*. Tolstoy, *War and Peace* (-1869).

YEAR	AGE	THE LIFE AND THE LAND
1865	8/9	American Civil War: Confederates surrender at Appomattox; Lincoln assassinated 5 days later; Andrew Johnson becomes President. 13th Amendment to US Constitution abolishes slavery. Reconstruction begins. Klu Klux Klan founded.
1870	13/14	Wilson family moves to Columbia, SC.
1873	16/17	Attends Davidson College, NC.
1874	17/18	Wilson family moves to Wilmington, NC; leaves Davidson and returns home
1875	18/19	Matriculates at College of New Jersey (Princeton University); later becomes member of Phi Kappa Psi fraternity.
1876	19/20	Sophomore at Princeton. Nov: Disputed presidential election; Rutherford Hayes becomes president-elect after protests.
1877	20/21	Junior at Princeton. Reconstruction ends in South.

	HISTORY	CULTURE
1865	Transatlantic telegraph cable completed.	Lewis Carroll, *Alice's Adventures in Wonderland*. Wagner, opera 'Tristan und Isolde'. The Queensbury Rules governing boxing are first outlined.
1870	Franco-Prussian War: Napoleon III defeated at Sedan. Italians enter Rome and declare it their capital.	Death of Charles Dickens. Jules Verne, *Twenty Thousand Leagues Under the Sea*.
1873	Germans evacuate last troops from France.	Tolstoy, *Anna Karenina*.
1874	End of Ashanti War. Britain annexes Fiji Islands.	Thomas Hardy, *Far from the Madding Crowd*.
1875	Risings in Bosnia and Herzegovina against Turkish rule. Britain buys Suez Canal shares from Khedive of Egypt.	Mark Twain, *The Adventures of Tom Sawyer*. Gilbert and Sullivan, operetta 'Trial by Jury'.
1876	Massacre of Bulgarians by Turkish troops. Ottoman sultan deposed. Serbia and Montenegro declare war on Ottoman Empire.	Henry James, *Roderick Hudson*. First complete performance of Wagner's 'Ring Cycle' at Bayreuth.
1877	Outbreak of Russo-Turkish War. Satsuma rebellion suppressed in Japan.	Henry James, *The American*. Rodin, sculpture 'The Age of Bronze'.

YEAR	AGE	THE LIFE AND THE LAND
1878	21/22	Senior at Princeton: graduates B.A.
1879	22/23	Further studies at University of Virginia Law School. Father serves as Moderator of PCUS.
1880	23/24	Dec: Leaves Virginia Law School and returns to family home.
1881	24/25	Studies law at home. President Garfield assassinated.
1882	25/26	Begins law practice as partner in Renick & Wilson, Atlanta, GA.
1883	26/27	Abandons law practice; engagement to Ellen Axson; begins postgraduate study at Johns Hopkins University.
1884	27/28	Works on first book.
1885	28/29	Jan: Congressional Government published. Jun: Marries Ellen Axson; accepts post at Bryn Mawr College, PA.

	HISTORY	CULTURE
1878	Russo-Turkish War. Congress of Berlin discusses Eastern Question.	Thomas Hardy, *The Return of the Native*. Algernon Charles Swinburne, *Poems and Ballads*.
1879	Zulu War. Alsace-Lorraine declared an integral part of Germany.	Henry James, *Daisy Miller*. Tchaikovsky, opera 'Eugen Onegin'.
1880	Transvaal Republic declares independence from Britain.	Death of George Eliot. Dostoevsky, *The Brothers Karamazov*.
1881	First Boer War. Pogroms against the Jews in Russia.	Henry James, *Portrait of a Lady*.
1882	Triple Alliance between Italy, Germany and Austria-Hungary. British occupy Cairo.	R L Stevenson, *Treasure Island*. Tchaikovsky, '1812 Overture'.
1883	The French gain control of Tunis. British decide to evacuate the Sudan.	Death of Wagner. Nietzsche, *Thus Spake Zarathustra*.
1884	General Gordon arrives in Khartoum. Germans occupy South-West Africa.	Mark Twain, *Huckleberry Finn*. *Oxford English Dictionary* begins publication (-1928).
1885	General Gordon killed in fall of Khartoum to the Mahdi. Germany annexes Tanganyika and Zanzibar.	Maupassant, *Bel Ami*. H Rider Haggard, *King Solomon's Mines*. Gilbert and Sullivan, operetta 'The Mikado'.

YEAR	AGE	THE LIFE AND THE LAND
1886	29/30	PhD awarded by Johns Hopkins for *Congressional Government*; birth of first daughter, Margaret.
1887	30/31	Birth of second daughter, Jessie.
1888	31/32	Leaves Bryn Mawr for Wesleyan University, CT; begins guest lectures at Johns Hopkins; mother dies.
1889	32/33	The State published; birth of third daughter, Eleanor.
1890	33/34	Appointed Professor of Jurisprudence and Political Economy, Princeton University.
1893	26/37	*Division and Revision, 1829–1889* published.
1896	39/40	*George Washington* published; suffers ill-health; travels to UK; delivers commencement address, 'Princeton in the Nation's Service'.
1898	41/42	Spanish-American War: US gains Cuba, Puerto Rico, Guam and the Philippines.

	HISTORY	CULTURE
1886	Irish Home Rule Bill introduced by Prime Minister Gladstone. Canadian-Pacific Railway completed.	R L Stevenson, *Dr Jekyll and Mr Hyde.* Rodin, sculpture 'The Kiss'.
1887	Queen Victoria's Golden Jubilee. Failed coup by General Boulanger in Paris.	Arthur Conan Doyle, *A Study in Scarlet.* Verdi, opera 'Otello'.
1888	Kaiser Wilhelm II accedes to the throne. Suez Canal convention.	Rudyard Kipling, *Plain Tales from the Hills.* Van Gogh, painting 'The Yellow Chair'.
1889	Austro-Hungarian Crown Prince Rudolf commits suicide at Mayerling.	Jerome K Jerome, *Three Men in a Boat.*
1890	Bismarck dismissed by Wilhelm II. Britain exchanges Heligoland with Germany for Zanzibar and Pemba.	Oscar Wilde, *The Picture of Dorian Gray.* First moving picture shows in New York.
1893	Franco-Russian alliance signed.	Oscar Wilde, *A Woman of No Importance.*
1896	Failure of Jameson Raid: Kaiser Wilhelm II sends 'Kruger Telegram'. Kitchener begins reconquest of the Sudan.	Chekhov, *The Seagull.* Nobel Prizes established.
1898	Kitchener defeats Mahdists at Omdurman. Death of Bismarck.	Thomas Hardy, *Wessex Poems.*

YEAR	AGE	THE LIFE AND THE LAND
1901	44/45	US President McKinley is assassinated: Theodore Roosevelt sworn in as President.
1902	45/46	Elected president of Princeton. USA acquires perpetual control over Panama Canal.
1903	46/47	1 Jan: Death of father. Wright Brothers' first flight.
1904	47/48	Initiates reforms at Princeton. Nov: Theodore Roosevelt wins US Presidential election.
1906	49/50	Feb: George Harvey proposes Wilson as future candidate for the presidency. May: Suffers ill health and briefly loses sight in one eye; recuperates in Lake District. San Francisco earthquake
1907	50/51	Jan: Holidays alone in Bermuda; possible affair with Mary Peck; conflict with Board of Trustees over further reforms at Princeton.

	HISTORY	CULTURE
1901	Death of Queen Victoria: succeeded by Edward VII. Negotiations for Anglo-German alliance end without agreement.	Thomas Mann, *Die Buddenbrooks.* Rudyard Kipling, *Kim.*
1902	Anglo-Japanese treaty recognises the independence of China and Korea. Triple Alliance between Austria, Germany and Italy renewed for another six years.	Arthur Conan Doyle, *The Hound of the Baskervilles.* Monet, 'Waterloo Bridge'.
1903	Beginning of Anglo-French Entente Cordiale.	Henry James, *The Ambassadors.* Film: *The Great Train Robbery.*
1904	Entente Cordiale settles Anglo-French colonial differences. Outbreak of Russo-Japanese War.	J M Barrie, *Peter Pan.* Freud, *The Psychopathology of Everyday Life.*
1906	Edward VII of England and Kaiser Wilhelm II of Germany meet. Britain grants self-government to Transvaal and Orange River Colonies.	John Galsworthy, *A Man of Property.* Invention of first jukebox.
1907	Dominion status granted to New Zealand. Peace Conference held in The Hague.	Joseph Conrad, *The Secret Agent.*

YEAR	AGE	THE LIFE AND THE LAND
1908	51/52	Jan: Again holidays alone in Bermuda; *Constitutional Government in the United States* published. Nov: William H Taft elected US President.
1909	52/53	Controversy over graduate school building and funding, Princeton.
1910	53/54	May: Wilson loses battle over graduate school. Sep: Nominated Democratic candidate, governorship of New Jersey. Nov: Elected governor.
1911	54/55	Begins campaigning for presidential nomination; meets Edward M House.
1912	55/56	22 Jun: Theodore Roosevelt quits Republican Party and forms Progressive Party. Jul: Nominated Democratic candidate for the presidency. Nov: Elected president defeating Theodore Roosevelt and William H Taft.
1913	56/57	4 Mar: Inaugurated president; tariff and Federal Reserve legislation passed; 16th Amendment permits income tax; 17th Amendment permits direct election of senators.

	HISTORY	CULTURE
1908	*The Daily Telegraph* publishes remarks about German hostility towards England made by Kaiser Wilhelm II. Union of South Africa is established.	E M Forster, *A Room with a View.* Kenneth Grahame, *The Wind in the Willows.*
1909	State visits of Edward VII to Berlin and Rome. Anglo-German discussions on the control of Baghdad railway.	H G Wells, *Tono-Bungay*. Vasily Kandinksy paints first abstract paintings.
1910	King Edward VII dies; succeeded by George V. Liberals win British General Election.	E M Forster, *Howard's End.* Karl May, *Winnetou.*
1911	Arrival of German gunboat *Panther* in Agadir triggers international crisis. Italy declares war on Turkey.	D H Lawrence, *The White Peacock.* Saki, *The Chronicles of Clovis.*
1912	The Liner *Titanic* sinks; 1,513 die. First Balkan War.	Alfred Adler, *The Nervous Character.* C G Jung, *The Theory of Psychoanalysis.*
1913	King George I of Greece assassinated and succeeded by Constantine I. Second Balkan War breaks out.	Marcel Proust, *Du côté de chez Swann.* Grand Central Station in New York is completed.

YEAR	AGE	THE LIFE AND THE LAND
1914	57/58	Apr: Orders US troops to Vera Cruz. 6 Aug: Death of Ellen Wilson. Sep/Oct: Further federal trade and anti-trust legislation.
1915	58/59	Mar: Meets Edith Bolling Galt. 7 May: Liner *Lusitania* sunk by German U-boat. 7 Jun: Bryan resigns as Secretary of State. 17 Jun: League to Enforce Peace founded. Sep: Announces engagement to Edith Galt. Dec: Marries Edith Galt.
1916	59/60	Mar: Pershing Expedition into Mexico in pursuit of Pancho Villa. May: Sends punitive expedition to Dominican Republic. Jun: National Defense Act passed. Nov: Re-elected president.
1917	60/61	22 Jan: Calls for *peace without victory*. 31 Jan: Germany declares unrestricted submarine warfare. 3 Feb: Breaks diplomatic links with Germany. 28 Feb: Publication of Zimmermann Telegram. 5 Mar: Second inauguration. 2 Apr: War address to Congress; establishes 'the Inquiry' to consider peace terms. 6 Apr: USA declares war on Germany. 14 Apr: Creel's CPI set up. May: Selective Service Act signed. 7 Jun: General Pershing and his staff arrive in England *en route* for France.

	HISTORY	CULTURE
1914	Archduke Franz Ferdinand of Austria-Hungary and his wife assassinated in Sarajevo. Outbreak of First World War.	James Joyce, *Dubliners.* Film: Charlie Chaplin in *Making a Living.*
1915	First World War: Battles of Neuve Chappelle and Loos. The 'Shells Scandal'. Gallipoli campaign.	John Buchan, *The Thirty-Nine Steps.* Film: *The Birth of a Nation.*
1916	First World War. Western Front: Battle of Verdun; Battle of the Somme. The Battle of Jutland. Lloyd George becomes British Prime Minister.	Lionel Curtis, *The Commonwealth of Nations.* James Joyce, *Portrait of an Artist as a Young Man.* Film: *Intolerance.*
1917	First World War. February Revolution in Russia. Nivelle offensive fails: mutinies in French army. Battle of Passchendaele (Third Ypres). British and Commonwealth forces take Jerusalem. Bolshevik take-over in Russia. German and Russian delegates sign armistice at Brest-Litovsk.	P G Wodehouse, *The Man With Two Left Feet.* T S Eliot, *Prufrock and Other Observations.* Film: *Easy Street.*

YEAR	AGE	THE LIFE AND THE LAND
1918	61/62	8 Jan: Delivers Fourteen Points address to Congress. Jul: Sends troops to Russia. Sep: American attack at St Mihiel; Meuse-Argonne offensive begins. 27 Sep: Calls for League of Nations to be integral part of peace treaty. 11 Nov: Armistice declared. Nov: Republican gains in congressional elections. 4 Dec: Sails for Europe aboard the *George Washington*.
1919	62/63	Jan: In Paris, following tour of Europe; Peace Conference opens. 6 Jan: Theodore Roosevelt dies. 14 Feb: draft of League Covenant presented. Feb-Mar: Returns briefly to US with draft Covenant of League, but defeated by Lodge's 'Round Robin'. 19 Feb: Attempt on Clemenceau's life. 7 May: Treaty presented to Germans – initially rejected. 28 Jun: Treaty of Versailles signed. 29 Jun: Leaves for the US. 10 Jul: Presents Treaty to Congress. Sep: Begins speaking tour but collapses in Pueblo, CO. 2 Nov: Suffers major stroke on return to Washington. 19 Nov: Treaty defeated in Senate. Wins Nobel Peace Prize.

	HISTORY	CULTURE
1918	First World War. Peace Treaty of Brest-Litovsk between Russia and the Central Powers. German Spring offensives on Western Front fail. Romania signs Peace of Bucharest with Germany and Austria-Hungary. Ex-Tsar Nicholas II and family executed. Kaiser Wilhelm II of German abdicates.	Gerald Manley Hopkins, *Poems.* Luigi Pirandello, *Six Characters in Search of an Author.*
1919	Communist Revolt in Berlin. Benito Mussolini founds fascist movement in Italy. Britain and France authorise resumption of commercial relations with Germany. British-Persian agreement at Tehran to preserve integrity of Persia. Irish War of Independence begins.	Bauhaus movement founded by Walter Gropius. George Bernard Shaw, *Heartbreak House.* Film: *The Cabinet of Dr Caligari.*

YEAR	AGE	THE LIFE AND THE LAND
1920	64/65	Attempts to save the League. 2 Nov: Warren Harding elected president with majority for the Republicans; 18th Amendment outlaws alcohol; 19th Amendment enfranchises women.
1921	64/65	Hands over to Harding; leaves White House for retirement. Washington Naval Treaty signed.
1924	67	3 Feb: Dies at home. Nov: Calvin Coolidge, Republican, wins US Presidential Election
1929		St Valentines Day Massacre of Chicago gangsters. the Wall Street Crash.
1930		The US, France, Italy, Japan and the UK sign the London Naval Treaty regulating naval expansion.

	HISTORY	CULTURE
1920	League of Nations comes into existence: headquarters moved to Geneva. Bolsheviks win Russian Civil War. Adolf Hitler announces his 25-point programme in Munich.	F Scott Fitzgerald, *This Side of Paradise.* Franz Kafka, *The Country Doctor.* Rambert School of Ballet formed.
1921	Paris Conference of wartime allies fixes Germany's reparation payments. Peace treaty signed between Russia and Germany.	D H Lawrence, *Women in Love.*
1924	Death of Lenin. Dawes Plan published. Nazi party enters the Reichstag for the first time.	Noel Coward, *The Vortex.* E M Forster, *A Passage to India.* Thomas Mann, *The Magic Mountain.*
1929	Fascists win single-party elections in Italy. Germany accepts Young Plan at Reparations Conference in the Hague – Allies agree to evacuate the Rhineland.	Ernest Hemingway, *A Farewell to Arms.* Erich Remarque, *All Quiet on the Western Front.*
1930	Nazi party in Germany gains 107 Reichstag seats. British Imperial Conference held in London: the Statute of Westminster is approved.	T S Eliot, *Ash Wednesday.* W H Auden, *Poems.* Noel Coward, *Private Lives.*

YEAR	AGE	THE LIFE AND THE LAND
1932		Stimson Doctrine. F D Roosevelt wins US Presidential election in Democrat landslide.
1933		Geneva Disarmament Conference collapses.
1935		US passes first Neutrality Act, prohibiting loans and sales of arms to belligerent nations.
1939		Following outbreak of Second World War, US revises Neutrality Acts to allow it to give financial and material aid to Great Britain.

	HISTORY	CULTURE
1932	Kurt von Schleicher forms ministry in Germany attempting to conciliate Centre and Left. Britain, France, Germany and Italy make the 'No Force' declaration.	Aldous Huxley, *Brave New World.* Films: *Grand Hotel. Tarzan the Ape Man.*
1933	Adolf Hitler is appointed Chancellor of Germany. Japan announces it will leave the League of Nations. Germany withdraws from League of Nations and Disarmament Conference.	George Orwell, *Down and Out in Paris and London.* Duke Ellington's Orchestra debuts in Britain. Films: *Duck Soup. King Kong. Queen Christina.*
1935	Saar is incorporated into Germany following a plebiscite. Hoare-Laval Pact. League of Nations imposes sanctions against Italy following its invasion of Abyssinia.	George Gershwin, *Porgy and Bess.* T S Eliot, *Murder in the Cathedral.* Films: *The 39 Steps. Top Hat.*
1939	Germans troops enter Prague. Germany demands Danzig and Polish Corridor. Poland refuses. Nazi-Soviet Pact. German invasion of Poland: Britain and France declare war. Soviets invade Finland.	James Joyce, *Finnegan's Wake.* John Steinbeck, *The Grapes of Wrath.* Films: *Gone with the Wind. Goodbye Mr Chips. The Wizard of Oz.*

YEAR	AGE	THE LIFE AND THE LAND
1941		7 Dec: Japan attacks US Pacific Fleet at Pearl Harbor and later invades the Philippines. Germany and Italy declare war on the USA. USA enters Second World War. Atomic bomb development begins in USA.

	HISTORY	CULTURE
1941	Second World War. British troops evacuate Greece: fall of Crete. Germany invades USSR Japanese troops occupy Indochina. Germans besiege Leningrad and Moscow. Soviets counter-attack at Moscow.	Bertold Brecht, *Mother Courage and Her Children.* Noel Coward, *Blithe Spirit.* Films: *Citizen Kane. Dumbo. The Maltese Falcon.*

Further Reading

The Wilson bibliography is vast and more than usually problematic, given the high proportion of medico-psychological theories among the published biographies. Blame for this rests squarely with the disaffected Wilson aide William C Bullitt, who collaborated with Sigmund Freud to produce *Thomas Woodrow Wilson: A Psychological Study* (Boston: 1967), an intriguing but pernicious account that depoliticises and decontextualises some of the main events and decisions in Wilson's life and which has continued to exert an influence on biographers to this day.

Though on different scales, former press secretary Ray Stannard Baker's *Woodrow Wilson: Life and Letters* (8 volumes, Garden City, NY: 1927–39) is attractively *parti pris*, while Wilson's brother-in-law Stockton Axson's *'Brother Woodrow': A Memoir of Woodrow Wilson* (Princeton, NJ: 1993) is warm enough to counter Bullitt and Freud but occasionally self-serving. Jan Willem Schulte Nordholt's *Woodrow Wilson: A Life for World Peace* (Berkeley/LA: 1991) is a very readable but rather literary exploration.

The doyen of Wilson studies was Arthur S Link (1922–98) whose detailed editorial work on *The Papers of Woodrow*

Wilson (69 volumes, Princeton, NJ: 1966–94) represents the most important research effort on the President's life and career, unlikely to be superseded. Link's five-volume *Wilson* (Princeton, NJ: 1947–65) consists of *The Road to the White House* (1947); *The New Freedom* (1956); *The Struggle for Neutrality, 1914–1915* (1960); *Confusions and Crises, 1915–1916* (1964); *Campaigns for Progressivism and Peace, 1916–1917* (1965), and remains the standard life.

On Wilson as peacemaker, Thomas A Bailey's poignantly titled *Woodrow Wilson and the Great Betrayal* (New York: 1947) and *Woodrow Wilson and the Lost Peace* (Chicago: 1963) are very valuable, as are John Milton Cooper Jr's *Breaking the Heart of the World: Woodrow Wilson and the Fight for the League of Nations* (Cambridge: 2001) and Thomas J Knock's *To End All Wars: Woodrow Wilson and the Quest for a New World Order* (New York: 1992) which proposes important later contexts for Wilsonian diplomacy.

No less fascinating and no less self-serving are a number of books which deal with or touch on, or in the case of A L and J L George's *Woodrow Wilson and Colonel House: A Personality Study* (New York: 1956), directly compare the President and his chief negotiator at the Peace Conference. Inga Floto's *Colonel House in Paris: A Study of American Policy at the Paris Peace Conference 1919* (Princeton, NJ: 1980) is crisply and authoritatively done, while Edward M House and C Seymour (eds), *What Really Happened at Paris: The Story of the Peace Conference, 1918–1919, by American delegates* (New York: 1921) makes only a lame protest of objectivity.

The best general account of the Paris Peace Conference is Margaret MacMillan's award-winning *Peacemakers: The Paris Conference of 1919 and Its Attempt to End War* (London: 2001) which is rich and entertaining, though not so straightforwardly organised as to provide a quick narrative. For more detailed study, one still needs to turn to H W V Temperley's six-volume *A History of the Peace Conference of Paris* (6 volumes, London: 1920–4), which I first encountered as a student 32 years ago and which obsesses me still. John Maynard Keynes's *The Economic Consequences of the Peace* (London: 1919) and Harold Nicholson's overquoted *Peacemaking, 1919* (London: 1964) are period pieces now and perhaps best left on the shelf.

For shorter introductions to Wilson's life, career and ideas, one can't do better than H W Brands' *Woodrow Wilson* (New York: 2003), which manages to be vividly detailed over a deceptively short span, or, better still, John A Thompson, *Profiles in Power* volume (London: 2002), which is learned, acute and very readable. It is a measure of Wilson's immensity in 20th century history that has attracted as much profound intelligence and solid effort as he has malice and mystification.

Picture Sources

The author and publishers wish to express their thanks to the following sources of illustrative material and/or permission to reproduce it. They will make proper acknowledgements in future editions in the event that any omissions have occurred.

Topham Picturepoint: pp. viii, 26, 130.

Endpapers

The Signing of Peace in the Hall of Mirrors, Versailles, 28th June 1919 by Sir William Orpen (Bridgeman Art Library)
Front Row: Dr Johannes Bell (Germany) signing with Herr Hermann Müller leaning over him
Middle row (seated, left to right): General Tasker H Bliss, Col E M House, Mr Henry White, Mr Robert Lansing, President Woodrow Wilson (United States); M Georges Clemenceau (France); Mr David Lloyd George, Mr Andrew Bonar Law, Mr Arthur J Balfour, Viscount Milner, Mr G N Barnes (Great Britain); Prince Saionji (Japan)
Back row (left to right): M Eleftherios Venizelos (Greece); Dr Afonso Costa (Portugal); Lord Riddell (British Press);

Sir George E Foster (Canada); M Nikola Pašić (Serbia); M Stephen Pichon (France); Col Sir Maurice Hankey, Mr Edwin S Montagu (Great Britain); the Maharajah of Bikaner (India); Signor Vittorio Emanuele Orlando (Italy); M Paul Hymans (Belgium); General Louis Botha (South Africa); Mr W M Hughes (Australia)

Jacket images

(Front): akg Images.
(Back): *Peace Conference at the Quai d'Orsay* by Sir William Orpen (akg Images).
Left to right (seated): Signor Orlando (Italy); Mr Robert Lansing, President Woodrow Wilson (United States); M Georges Clemenceau (France); Mr David Lloyd George, Mr Andrew Bonar Law, Mr Arthur J Balfour (Great Britain); Left to right (standing): M Paul Hymans (Belgium); Mr Eleftherios Venizelos (Greece); The Emir Feisal (The Hashemite Kingdom); Mr W F Massey (New Zealand); General Jan Smuts (South Africa); Col E M House (United States); General Louis Botha (South Africa); Prince Saionji (Japan); Mr W M Hughes (Australia); Sir Robert Borden (Canada); Mr G N Barnes (Great Britain); M Ignacy Paderewski (Poland)

Index

NB All family relationships are to Woodrow Wilson unless otherwise stated.

R

S

T

V

W

UK PUBLICATION: November 2008 to December 2010
CLASSIFICATION: Biography/History/
International Relations
FORMAT: 198 × 128mm
EXTENT: 208pp
ILLUSTRATIONS: 6 photographs plus 4 maps
TERRITORY: world

Chronology of life in context, full index, bibliography innovative layout with sidebars

Woodrow Wilson: United States of America by Brian Morton
Friedrich Ebert: Germany by Harry Harmer
Georges Clemenceau: France by David Watson
David Lloyd George: Great Britain by Alan Sharp
Prince Saionji: Japan by Jonathan Clements
Wellington Koo: China by Jonathan Clements
Eleftherios Venizelos: Greece by Andrew Dalby
From the Sultan to Atatürk: Turkey by Andrew Mango
The Hashemites: The Dream of Arabia by Robert McNamara
Chaim Weizmann: The Dream of Zion by Tom Fraser
Piip, Meierovics & Voldemaras: Estonia, Latvia & Lithuania by Charlotte Alston
Ignacy Paderewski: Poland by Anita Prazmowska
Beneš, Masaryk: Czechoslovakia by Peter Neville
Károlyi & Bethlen: Hungary by Bryan Cartledge
Karl Renner: Austria by Jamie Bulloch
Vittorio Orlando: Italy by Spencer Di Scala
Pašić & Trumbić: The Kingdom of Serbs, Croats and Slovenes by Dejan Djokic
Aleksandŭr Stamboliĭski: Bulgaria by R J Crampton
Ion Bratianu: Romania by Keith Hitchin
Paul Hymans: Belgium by Sally Marks
General Smuts: South Africa by Antony Lentin
William Hughes: Australia by Carl Bridge
William Massey: New Zealand by James Watson
Sir Robert Borden: Canada by Martin Thornton
Maharajah of Bikaner: India by Hugh Purcell
Afonso Costa: Portugal by Filipe Ribeiro de Meneses
Epitácio Pessoa: Brazil by Michael Streeter
South America by Michael Streeter
Central America by Michael Streeter
South East Asia by Andrew Dalby
The League of Nations by Ruth Henig
Consequences of Peace: The Versailles Settlement – Aftermath and Legacy by Alan Sharp